DATE DUE	
NOV 0 2 1998	
NOV 2 4 1998	
AUG 27 1999	
NOV 2 2 1999	
DEC 0 5 2000	
MAR 9 2001	
APR 2 3 2003	
NOV 0 6 2003	
FEB 1 6 2004	
APR 1 5 2004	
MAR 0 8 2005	

Saints

for
young Readers
for every day

Second Edition
Volume 2
July–December

Revised and Edited by
Susan Helen Wallace, fsp

Illustrated by
Jamie H. Aven

Pauline
BOOKS & MEDIA
BOSTON

Saints for young readers for every day / revised and edited by Susan Helen Wallace. — 2nd ed.
       p.   cm.
     Includes indexes.
     ISBN 0-8198-6970-8 (set : hardcover). — ISBN 0-8198-6971-6 (set : pbk.). — ISBN 0-8198-6966-X (v. 1 : hardcover). — ISBN 0-8198-6967-8 (v. 1 pbk.). — ISBN 0-8198-6968-6 (v. 2 : hardcover). — ISBN 0-8198-6969-4 (v. 2 : pbk.).
     1. Christian saints—Biography—Juvenile literature. [1. Saints.]   I. Wallace, Susan Helen, 1940-
BX4653.D34   1994
282' .092'2—dc20
[B]   94-11927
                                                                       CIP
                                                                        AC

Cover Illustration by Elinor Kaslow

Printed and published in the U.S.A. by Pauline Books & Media, 50 St. Paul's Avenue, Boston, MA 02130.

http://www.pauline.org   E-mail: PBM_EDIT@INTERRAMP.COM

Pauline Books & Media is the publishing house of the Daughters of St. Paul, an international congregation of women religious serving the Church with the communications media.

 2 3 4 5 6 7 8 9 10   06 05 04 03 02 01 00 99 98 97

I dedicate this volume of *Saints for Young Readers for Every Day* to my father, Leo Wallace, who introduced me as a child to the saints. He told me the story of their lives and gave me books of saints to read and cherish. Dad died on December 29, 1993, the feast of one of his favorite saints—Thomas Becket. To Dad, and all the parents like my parents, who gave more than physical life to their children, may this book be a small tribute.

How to Use this Book

This book is the second volume of a two-part set. Volume one covers January through June. Volume two covers July through December. You will find stories about saints. Some lived long lives; others died when they were young. You will discover that some were close to God from childhood and teenage years. Others learned the hard way that only God can make us happy.

You will meet saints from every nation and race. They are from different centuries, starting with the early days of the Church, right down to our own times. You will come to know saintly kings and laborers, queens and housemaids, popes and priests, nuns and religious brothers. They were mothers and fathers, teenagers and children. They were doctors and farmers, soldiers and lawyers.

Saints were not one type of person. They were as different from each other as we are. They were as human as we are. They lived on this earth, experienced temptations and faced problems. They became saints because they used their will power to make right choices and they prayed. They tried to correct their faults and they never gave up trusting in Jesus' love for them.

What is the best way to read this book? Do not try to read all the stories in a few days. Read the saints a day at a time. Most days have one saint to think about. A few days have more than one. The saint for the day is the saint from the current Roman calendar. When the calendar does not present a saint that day, we have gone to the previous calendar and have chosen a saint or blessed we thought you might appreciate being acquainted with. The saints and blesseds for North America are also included here.

You might ask what is the difference between a SAINT and a BLESSED. Saints are holy persons now in heaven who grew close to God while on earth. The Church declares them saints so that we can love, imitate and pray to them. Saints can pray to God for us and help us. Persons declared BLESSED are holy people who are now in heaven. Usually the Church requires miracles obtained through their intervention. When the miracles have been carefully studied and accepted as real, the blesseds are proclaimed saints. You will also meet MARTYRS in this book. Martyrs allowed themselves to be put to death rather than give up the Catholic faith.

Keep these true stories by your bedside and read the saint of the day before or after morning or evening prayers. In this way, you will be able to think about what you read throughout the day. Read also the brief recommendation at the end of each biography. Try to practice that suggestion. Slowly but surely you will see an improvement in yourself. And there is no telling where you may go from there. Maybe you, too, will become a saint. And why not?

Here is a friendly tip: if you find it hard to be the kind of person you want to be, why not ask the saint of that day to help you? By the end of the year you will have many wonderful friends. You might also want to read more biographies about the saints you especially liked.

Contents

July

august

septembeR

OCTOBER

NOVEMBER

δecembeR

JULY 1

BLESSED JUNIPERO SERRA

Junipero Serra was born in Petra, Spain, on November 24, 1713. The boy became a student at the Franciscan school in Palma, twenty-five miles away. He joined the Franciscan order on September 14, 1730, a few months before his seventeenth birthday. During the novitiate, Junipero read a biography of Franciscan saints. The saint whose life captivated him most was St. Francis Solano, who had lived from 1549 until 1610. This missionary priest to South America had just been declared a saint in 1726 by Pope Benedict XIII. The young novice decided that, if it was God's will, he too would be a missionary.

Junipero was ordained a priest in 1736. He became a professor of philosophy. After he had been in the order twenty years, he was given a wonderful opportunity. Franciscan friars were asked to volunteer for the mission territories called "New Spain" (Mexico and California). Junipero and his close friend, Friar Francisco Palou, joined the missionary band at Cadiz, Spain, a seaport city. From there they sailed the Atlantic Ocean to Vera Cruz, Mexico. They landed on December 6, 1749.

Junipero and another friar walked the next part of the journey from Vera Cruz to Mexico City, a distance of 240 miles. They began on December 15, 1749, and arrived on January 1, 1750. From Mexico City, Junipero and Friar Francisco Palou were sent to work among the Pame Indians at the Franciscan Mission of the Sierra Gorda.

Several of the friars were then assigned to missions in Lower California. Junipero, Francisco and a handful of other Franciscans were asked to bring the Gospel to the native peoples in Upper California. Junipero started Mission San Diego on July 16, 1769, when he was fifty-six years old. The mission was an open invitation to his beloved people to come and meet Jesus. Gradually, they trusted the friars. Some people were baptized and began to live the Christian faith. Father Serra and the friars loved and protected their people. The golden chain of new missions grew: Mission San Carlos in Monterey on June 1, 1770; Mission San Antonio de Padua on July 14, 1771; Mission San Gabriel Archangel, September 8, 1771; Mission San Luis Obispo, September 1, 1772; Mission San Francisco de Asis, October 9, 1776; Mission San Juan Capistrano, November 1, 1776; Mission Santa Clara de Asis, January 12, 1777; Mission San Buenaventura, March 31, 1782. Eventually, six thousand native peoples were baptized.

Blessed Junipero made his final tour of the missions in Upper California from the last part of 1783 until July of 1784. He died peacefully at Mission San Carlos on August 28, 1784, and is buried there. In 1988, Pope John Paul II declared Father Junipero Serra "blessed."

Advertisements keep telling us to take care of "number one." We can be selfish or too self-centered sometimes. Then we can ask Blessed Junipero Serra to give us some of his compassion and concern for others. We can also ask him to give us a bit of his missionary spirit.

JULY 2

ST. OTTO

Otto lived in the twelfth century. He was born in Swabia, present-day Bavaria. He became a priest and was assigned to the service of Emperor Henry IV. Eventually, Father Otto acquired a high state office. He became Henry's chancellor. Otto tried to influence the emperor to act justly and to be moderate in his decisions. But Henry committed crimes and tried to cause division in the Church. He even appointed his own pope. Otto felt very bad and worked to help Henry reform. Henry IV took it upon himself to appoint Otto a bishop. Otto refused to be consecrated until he could go to Rome and receive the approval of the true pope, Paschal II. The pope did consecrate him. Bishop Otto became a great help to the people of Swabia, especially under Emperor Henry V. This emperor followed the ways of his father, Henry IV. But although he was harsh and severe, he respected Otto and often listened to his advice.

When King Boleslaus III of Poland conquered part of Pomerania, he asked Otto to go there. Pomerania was a province of Prussia in the Baltic area. The people were pagans. Bishop Otto welcomed the opportunity to bring them the Good News. In 1124, the bishop led a group of priests and catechists into Pomerania. Many people were instructed and baptized. Some say the number of conversions was over twenty thousand. Bishop Otto assigned priests to minister to the new Christians. He returned to his own country. After a while, some of the people of Pomerania began to return to their old pagan ways. Bishop Otto went back to Pomerania in 1128. He helped the people become fervent Christians again. He died on June 30, 1139, and was proclaimed a saint by Pope Clement III in 1189.

It is easy sometimes to think that we can do wrong things because everyone else does. But St. Otto teaches us by his life that we have to be courageous enough to do something good when we can or to say "no" when something is wrong. We can pray to him to help us.

JULY 3

ST. THOMAS

Thomas was one of the twelve apostles of Jesus. His name in the Syriac language means "twin." St. Thomas loved Jesus greatly, even though at first his belief was not very strong. Once when Jesus was going to face the danger of being killed, the other apostles tried to keep the Master back. St. Thomas said to them, "Let us also go, that we may die with him."

When Jesus was captured by his enemies, Thomas lost his courage. He ran away with the other apostles. His heart was broken with sorrow at the death of his beloved Lord. Then on Easter Sunday, Jesus appeared to his apostles after he had risen from the dead. Thomas was not with them at the time. As soon as he arrived, the other apostles told him joyfully, "We have seen the Lord." They thought Thomas would be happy. Instead, he did not believe their message.

"Unless I see in his hands the print of the nails," he said, "and put my finger in the place of the nails, and put my hand into his side, I will not believe." Eight days later, Jesus appeared to his apostles again. This time, Thomas was there, too. Christ called him and told him to touch his hands and the wound in his side. Poor St. Thomas! He fell down at the Master's feet and cried out, "My Lord and my God!" Then Jesus said, "Because you have seen me, Thomas, you have believed. Blessed are they who have not seen, and yet have believed."

After Pentecost, Thomas was strong and firm in his belief and trust in Jesus. It is said that he went to India to preach the Gospel. He died a martyr there, after making many converts.

When the priest lifts the sacred Host at Mass, we too can pray the words of St. Thomas, "My Lord and my God!"

JULY 4

ST. ELIZABETH OF PORTUGAL

Elizabeth, a Spanish princess, was born in 1271. She married King Denis of Portugal at the age of twelve. Elizabeth was beautiful and very lovable. She was also devout and went to Mass every day. Elizabeth was a charming wife. Her husband was fond of her at first, but soon he began to cause her great suffering. Though a good ruler, he did not have his wife's love of prayer and virtue. In fact, his sins of impurity were well-known scandals throughout his kingdom.

St. Elizabeth tried to be a loving mother to her children, Alphonso and Constance. She was also generous and loving with the people of Portugal. Even though her husband was unfaithful, she prayed that he would have a change of heart. Elizabeth refused to become bitter and resentful. She strengthened her own prayer life and followed the Franciscan spirituality. Gradually, the king was moved by her patience and good example. He began to live better. He apologized to his wife and showed her greater respect. In his last sickness the queen never left his side, except for Mass. King Denis died on January 6, 1325. He had shown deep sorrow for his sins and his death was peaceful.

Elizabeth lived eleven more years. She performed loving acts of charity and penance. She was a wonderful model of kindness toward the poor. This gentle woman was also a peacemaker between members of her own family and between nations.

St. Elizabeth of Portugal died on July 4, 1336. She was proclaimed a saint by Pope Urban VIII in 1626.

St. Elizabeth found the strength for daily living at morning Mass. We can ask her to help us appreciate the great treasure of the Mass. She will also help us to participate often and devoutly at Mass.

JULY 5

ST. ANTHONY MARY ZACCARIA

Anthony was born in Italy in 1502. While he was still young, his father died. His mother encouraged Anthony in the special love he felt for the sufferings of poor people. Mrs. Zaccaria sent her son to the University of Padua so that he could become a doctor. He was only twenty-two when he graduated.

The young doctor was very successful. Yet he did not feel satisfied. He realized that he wanted to become a priest. Anthony began to study theology. He also continued to care for the sick, to comfort and inspire the dying. He started to use all his spare moments to read and meditate on the letters of St. Paul in the Bible. He had read the life of the great apostle Paul many times, and had given much thought to his virtues. Now Anthony was burning with a strong desire to become a saint and to bring everyone to Jesus.

After he was ordained a priest, St. Anthony Mary moved to the great city of Milan. There he would be able to help many more people. He also started an order of priests. They are the Clerks Regular of St. Paul. People call them "Barnabites" after their headquarters at the Church of St. Barnabas in Milan. In imitation of the apostle Paul, St. Anthony and his priests preached everywhere. They repeated the words and sentences of Paul. They explained Paul's message with words that were easy to understand. The people loved and appreciated this. St. Anthony also had a great love for Jesus in the Blessed Sacrament. In fact, he started the practice of the Forty Hours Devotion.

St. Anthony Mary was only thirty-seven when he died on July 5, 1539. Pope Leo XIII proclaimed him a saint in 1897.

St. Anthony Mary Zaccaria used to say, "I have never asked St. Paul for a grace without having received it." In imitation of St. Anthony Mary, let us ask St. Paul for the grace we need the most.

ST. MARIA GORETTI

Maria was born in 1890. Her father died when she and the other five children in her family were small. At twelve, Maria was already very pretty. She helped her mother on the farm, in the house and with the care of the other children. She never complained because they were so poor. In fact, she cheered up her poor mother and was a great comfort to her. She went to Mass regularly even though it meant a two-hour walk. Maria also received the sacrament of Reconciliation as often as she could.

A young neighbor, Alexander, tried a few times to make Maria sin. She absolutely refused. She did her best to avoid him. July 5, 1902, was a hot summer day. Maria was alone in the cottage mending clothes. Alexander came again to try to make her sin. He dragged her into a room. When she tried to scream, he stuffed a handkerchief into her mouth. Yet Maria managed to keep saying, "No, no! It is a mortal sin. God doesn't want it. If you commit it, you will go to hell." And she struggled as much as she could. Alexander panicked. He stabbed her furiously with a dagger. Then he ran away.

Maria was taken to a hospital, where she died about twenty-four hours later. During her last hours, she forgave her murderer. Her only worry

was for her mother. With great joy, the girl received Jesus in Holy Communion. Then she went to heaven. Alexander was sent to prison. For a long time, he did not repent of his horrible crime. Then one night he had a dream or vision of Maria offering him flowers. From that moment on, he was a changed man. When he was freed from prison after twenty-seven years, his first visit was to the Goretti home. He asked Maria's mother for forgiveness. Then Alexander spent the rest of his life as the gardener in a nearby monastery.

Maria was declared "blessed" by Pope Pius XII on April 27, 1947. He appeared on the balcony of St. Peter's with Maria's eighty-two-year-old mother, Assunta. Three years later, on July 25, 1950, the same pope declared Maria a saint. He called her "a martyr of holy purity."

We can help ourselves live our Christian values if we participate in the Mass and receive the sacrament of Reconciliation. We can also choose good movies, videos, books and magazines. When we feel weak, we can ask St. Maria Goretti to help us be the kind of Christian she was.

BLESSED ROGER DICKENSON, BLESSED RALPH MILNER AND BLESSED LAWRENCE HUMPHREY

These three martyrs lived in England during the time of Church persecution by Queen Elizabeth I. "Mr." Roger Dickenson was an undercover diocesan priest. Ralph Milner was a husband and father. He worked as a farm laborer and was brought into the Church through the good example of his neighbors. The day he made his First Communion he was put into prison for being a Catholic. The jailer liked Mr. Milner so his prison confinement was not strict at first. For several years, he went on "parole" to find supplies of food and whatever the other prisoners needed. While on parole, he was of great help to "Mr." Dickenson and Father Stanney, a Jesuit. The day came when Father Dickenson, too, was caught. He and Mr. Milner were brought to trial together. Father Dickenson was tried for the crime of being a Catholic priest. Mr. Milner was tried for helping Father Dickenson perform his ministry. The judge looked at the crowd in the courtroom. He thought of Mrs. Milner and the couple's eight children. He wanted to free Milner at all costs. "All you have to do," he said, "is visit a Protestant church, just for a few minutes, to say you have been there. I'll let you go free to be with your family." Mr. Milner quietly and firmly refused. He and Father Dickenson went bravely to their deaths. It was July 7, 1591.

The third martyr, Lawrence Humphrey, had been brought into the Church by Father Stanney, S.J. He would not give up the faith he had so recently acquired. Lawrence was just twenty-one years old when he was martyred.

Every martyr reminds us that a treasure is worth defending. The martyrs recognized the value of their Catholic religion. They would not give it up for any reason. We can pray to Blessed Roger, Blessed Ralph and Blessed Lawrence. They will lead us to love and cherish our beliefs as they did.

JULY 8

BLESSED EUGENE III

Blessed Eugene III was born near Pisa, Italy, in the twelfth century. He was baptized Peter. St. Antoninus, whose feast day is May 10, called Pope Eugene "a great pope with great sufferings."

Pope Eugene had been Father Peter, a priest in Pisa, when he felt the call to become a Cistercian monk. He went to Clairvaux, France, and joined the monks there. St. Bernard of Clairvaux was the superior. His feast day is August 20. Peter chose "Bernard" for his religious name. He did this because of his great esteem for St. Bernard.

St. Bernard sent his namesake, Bernard, to become the superior of a monastery in Rome. Pope Lucius II died in 1145. That is when a most unusual thing happened. The cardinals elected Abbot Bernard to be pope. The abbot was not at the meeting because he was not a cardinal. He was shocked. St. Bernard of Clairvaux was surprised too. He felt sorry for Bernard. He wrote an open letter to the cardinals: "May God forgive you for what you have done," he said. "You have involved in responsibilities and placed among many people a man who fled them both."

Bernard chose to be called Eugene III. His time as pope brought him many difficulties. The Roman senate threatened to oppose him if he did not let them keep stolen property. A man who had been previously excommunicated went to Pope Eugene and asked forgiveness. Soon after, he fell back into his old ways. He even joined a faction that was directly against the pope. Pope Eugene had to leave Rome a few times because of the dangers surrounding him. When this happened, he would find peace and strength at a monastery. Then he would have the courage to go back and face his difficult task again. He wore his Cistercian habit and lived simply. No matter how hectic his life was, he always had the heart of a monk. One of his fellow monks wrote to St. Bernard of Clairvaux about Pope Eugene: "There is no arrogance or domineering way in him." Pope Eugene died on July 8, 1153.

Some people want high positions because they like the power and glory. But those who are successful are

people like Blessed Eugene III who do not seek praise.
When we want everyone to notice and praise us, we can
ask Blessed Eugene to show us how to be humble.

JULY 9

THE MARTYRS OF ORANGE

The martyrs of Orange lived in the eighteenth century. They were thirty-two nuns. During the French Revolution, these sisters, from different religious orders, were jailed in Orange, France. There were sixteen Ursuline sisters, thirteen Sisters Adorers of the Blessed Sacrament, two Bernardine sisters and one Benedictine sister.

While the French Revolution raged, these nuns were told that they had to take an oath of loyalty to the leaders of the Revolution. The sisters believed that the oath was against God and the Church. Each refused to sign it and were taken to the Orange jail. Some of the sisters had lived in the same convents before they came to jail. Others did not know any of the sisters until they met in prison. The nuns formed a community in that dark, damp room. They prayed together at particular times during the day. They cheered up and consoled each other and bonded as the early persecuted Christian Church had. On July 6, the first sister was taken to trial and condemned to the guillotine. She never returned. Every day another sister, some days two sisters, were taken. No one knew who would be next. The group diminished in size, but the remaining sisters prayed especially for those who would die that day. Then they would sing a hymn of praise to God called the *Te Deum*.

By the end of July, 1794, thirty-two sisters had been condemned by the people's court at Orange, France. Thirty-two sisters were martyrs. When the French Revolution was over, the judges of Orange were convicted for what they had done. The thirty-two sisters called the martyrs of Orange were declared "blessed" by Pope Pius XI in 1925.

Sometimes we hear talk or see things going on that we know are not right. We can ask the martyrs of Orange to give us the courage to behave the way they would if they were in our place.

JULY 10

ST. FELICITY AND HER SEVEN SONS

Felicity was a noble Christian woman of Rome. She lived during the second century. After her husband's death, she served God by prayer and works of charity. Her good example led others to become Christians, too. This angered the pagan priests, who complained to Antoninus Pius, the emperor. They said Felicity was an enemy of the state because she was making the gods angry. So the emperor ordered Felicity arrested. Seven young men were arrested with her. It is believed that they were her sons. Like the mother of the Maccabees in the Old Testament, Felicity remained calm. The governor tried in vain to make her sacrifice to the gods. He ended with the words, "Unhappy woman, if you wish to die, die! But do not destroy your sons."

"My sons will live forever if, like me, they scorn the idols and die for their God," Felicity answered. This brave woman was forced to watch her sons being put to death. One was whipped, two were beaten with clubs, three beheaded and another drowned. Four months later, Felicity, too, was beheaded. Her strength came from her great hope that she would be with God and her sons in heaven.

St. Felicity, it could be said, was martyred eight different times. This is because she had to watch each of her sons die. Then she too gave up her life for Jesus.

Let us pray every day that God will bless our family and friends. May we all meet again in heaven.

JULY 11

ST. BENEDICT

St. Benedict was born in 480. He was from a rich Italian family. His life was full of adventure and wonderful deeds. As a boy, he was sent to Rome to study in the public schools. When he was a young man, he became disgusted with the corrupt lifestyle of pagan Rome. Benedict left the city and went looking for a place where he could be alone with God. He found the right spot. It was a cave in the mountain of Subiaco. Benedict spent three years there alone. The devil often tempted him to go back to his rich home and easy life. However, Benedict overcame these temptations by prayer and penance. One day, the devil kept making him think of a beautiful lady he had once seen in Rome. The devil tried to make him go back to look for that lady. Benedict almost gave in to the temptation. Then he felt so sorry that he threw himself into a bush of long, sharp thorns. He rolled around in the thorns until he was covered with scratches. From then on, his life was calm. He did not feel powerful temptations like that again.

After three years, people started coming to Benedict. They wanted to learn how to become holy. He became the leader of some men who asked for his help. But when he tried to make them do penance, they grew angry. It is said that the men even tried to poison Benedict. He made the

Sign of the Cross over the poisoned wine and the glass shattered to pieces.

Later, Benedict became the leader of many good monks. He started twelve monasteries. Then he went to Montecassino where he built his most well-known monastery. It was here that St. Benedict wrote the wonderful rules for the Benedictine order. He taught his monks to pray and work hard. He taught them especially to be humble always. Benedict and his monks greatly helped the people of their times. They taught them how to read and write, how to farm, and how to work at different trades. St. Benedict was able to do good because he prayed all the time. He died on March 21, 547. In 1966, Pope Paul VI proclaimed him the patron of Europe. In 1980, Pope John Paul II added St. Cyril and St. Methodius as patrons of Europe along with St. Benedict.

St. Benedict reminds us that there is a deep need in us to have some time for God. We don't have to go to a mountain cave, though. We can stop in at church and make a visit to Jesus in the Blessed Sacrament. We can also have a prayer corner in our room. We will grow close to God through our daily conversations with Jesus.

ST. JOHN GAULBERT

St. John was born in Florence, Italy, at the end of the tenth century. He and his father were devastated when John's only brother, Hugh, was murdered. The man who did it was supposed to have been Hugh's friend. Urged on by his father and by his own anger, John began looking for a way to avenge his brother's death. He felt that his personal honor depended on it.

One Good Friday, he came face to face with the murderer in a narrow passageway. John drew his sword and started toward the man. Hugh's killer fell to his knees. He crossed his arms on his chest and begged forgiveness for love of Jesus who died on the cross. With a tremendous effort, John dropped his sword. He embraced his enemy and moved on down the road. When he came to a monastery church, he went in and knelt before the crucifix. He asked forgiveness for his sins. Then a miracle happened! Christ on the cross bowed his head. It was as if to tell John that he was pleased with him for forgiving his enemy. John felt that his own sins were forgiven. Such a change came over him that he went straight to the abbot of that monastery. He asked if he could join the monks.

When John's father heard about it, he said he would burn the whole monastery if his son did not come out. The monks did not know what to do.

John solved the problem by cutting off his hair and borrowing a habit from one of the monks. Even his father was so impressed that he let him remain. St. John later went off to live a stricter life. He started his own community of monks.

John became a model for imitating the poor lifestyle of Jesus. He also took wonderful care of all the poor people who came to the monastery gate. God granted him power to work miracles and to give wise guidance. Even Pope St. Leo IX went to St. John to seek his advice. St. John died on July 12, 1073. He was proclaimed a saint by Pope Celestine III in 1193.

Even the greatest sins can be forgiven by God. If we forgive those who do wrong to us, God will also forgive our sins. We can ask St. John Gaulbert to help us have forgiving hearts like his.

JULY 13

ST. HENRY II

Henry was born in 972. He became the duke of Bavaria in 995. One night he had an unusual vision. St. Wolfgang, who had been his beloved teacher when he was a boy, appeared to him. Wolfgang pointed to the words, "after six" written on the wall. What could that mean? Perhaps Henry was to die in six days? With that thought, he prayed with great fervor for six days. At the end of the six days, however, he was in perfect health. Perhaps it meant six months? The duke devoted himself to doing good more than ever. At the end of six months, he was healthier than before. So he decided he had six years to get ready for death. But instead of dying after that time had passed, he was elected emperor of Germany. Then he understood what the vision had meant.

Henry worked hard to keep his people happy and at peace. To defend justice he had to fight many wars. He was honest in battle and insisted that his armies be honorable too. Henry married a very gentle and loving woman named Cunegundes (or Kunigunda) around 998. She, too, has been proclaimed a saint. Henry and Cunegundes went to Rome in 1014. They were crowned emperor and empress of the Holy Roman Empire. It was a great honor because Pope Benedict VIII himself crowned them.

Emperor Henry was one of the best rulers of the Holy Roman Empire. He promoted Church reform. He encouraged the growth of new monasteries and built beautiful churches. He showed his own love for Jesus and the Church with sincerity and love. He was a man of prayer and was greatly attracted to religious life. But he accepted his role as husband and ruler and fulfilled his responsibilities generously. Henry was just fifty-two when he died in 1024. He was proclaimed a saint by Blessed Eugene III in 1146. Pope St. Pius X named Emperor Henry the patron of Benedictine Oblates.

Emperor Henry reminds us that we can never say we are too busy to give time to God. Who was more busy than Emperor Henry? We can ask him to help us keep our priorities straight.

BLESSED KATERI TEKAKWITHA

Between the years 1642 and 1649, St. Isaac Jogues and the North American martyrs came from France. They were killed while evangelizing the Indians. Ten years after the death of St. Isaac Jogues, Kateri Tekakwitha was born in the same village where he had died. (We celebrate the feast of St. Isaac and the North American Martyrs on October 19.)

Kateri means Katherine. Kateri was born in Auriesville, New York, in 1656. Her mother was a Christian Algonquin. Her father was a non-Christian Mohawk chief. Kateri's parents died of smallpox when the girl was fourteen. A Mohawk uncle raised her. This is how Kateri met the missionaries. On one occasion, her uncle had three Jesuit missionaries as his guests. Kateri began to receive instructions in the faith. She was baptized on Easter Sunday, 1676. That is when she took the name Kateri.

The village in which she lived was not Christian. In fact, in her lodge there was not one other

Christian. The Indians did not appreciate her choice to remain unmarried. They insulted her and some resented that she did not work on Sunday. But Kateri held her ground. She prayed her Rosary every day, even when others made fun of her. She practiced patience and suffered quietly. Kateri's life grew harder. Some people were so harsh that their treatment was a persecution. She fled to a Christian village near Montreal. There on Christmas Day, 1677, she received her First Communion. It was a wonderful day. Father Pierre Cholonec, a Jesuit, guided her spiritual life for the next three years. She and an older Iroquois woman named Anastasia lived as joyful, generous Christians. Kateri made a private vow of virginity on March 25, 1679. She was just twenty-four when she died on April 17, 1680. Exactly three hundred years later, on June 22, 1980, Kateri Tekakwitha was declared "blessed" by Pope John Paul II.

Blessed Kateri received the gift of belief in Jesus because of the sacrifices of the missionaries. We can thank Jesus for those who brought the Catholic religion into our lives, too. Who are they? Our parents? Grandparents? Other relatives? Parish priest? Religion teacher? We can ask Blessed Kateri to teach us how to be grateful by sharing our faith with others.

JULY 15

ST. BONAVENTURE

Bonaventure's name means "good luck." He was born in 1221 in Tuscany, Italy, and was baptized John. Bonaventure joined the Franciscan order, which was still new. In fact, St. Francis of Assisi who started the Franciscans lived from 1181 until 1226. Francis was still alive when Bonaventure was born. As a young Franciscan, Bonaventure left his own country to study at the University of Paris in France. He became a wonderful writer about the things of God. He loved God so much that people began to call him the "Seraphic Doctor." Seraphic means angelic.

One of Bonaventure's famous friends was St. Thomas Aquinas. His feast day is January 28. Thomas asked Bonaventure where he got all the beautiful things he wrote. St. Bonaventure took his friend and led him to his desk. He pointed to the large crucifix which always stood on his desk. "It is he who tells me everything. He is my only Teacher." Another time when Bonaventure was writing the life of St. Francis of Assisi, he was so full of fervor that St. Thomas exclaimed: "Let us leave a saint to write about a saint." St. Bonaventure always kept himself humble even though his books made him famous.

In 1265, Pope Clement IV wanted him to become an archbishop. Bonaventure begged the pope to accept his refusal. The pope respected his decision. However, Bonaventure did agree to be master general of his order. This difficult task was his for seventeen years. In 1273, Blessed Pope Gregory X made Bonaventure a cardinal. The two papal messengers found Bonaventure at the large wash tubs. He was taking his turn scrubbing the pots and pans. The papal messengers waited patiently until Bonaventure finished the last pot. He rinsed and dried his hands. Then they solemnly presented him the large red hat which symbolized his new honor.

Cardinal Bonaventure was a great help to this pope who had called the Council of Lyons in 1274. Thomas Aquinas died on his way to the Council, but Bonaventure made it. He was very influential at the assembly. Yet he, too, died rather suddenly on July 14, 1274, at the age of fifty-three. The pope was at his bedside when he died. Bonaventure was proclaimed a saint in 1482 by Pope Sixtus IV. In 1588, Pope Sixtus V declared him a Doctor of the Church.

We, too, should have a crucifix on our desk or in our room. Then we can turn often to Jesus for help and strength as St. Bonaventure did.

JULY 16

OUR LADY OF MOUNT CARMEL

Mount Carmel is a mountain overlooking the plain of Galilee. It became famous when the prophet Elijah, who lived before Our Lord, was born. Elijah worked a miracle there. Chapter 18 of the Bible's First Book of Kings tells how Elijah stood up to the 450 prophets of the false god Baal. Through his prayers, Elijah obtained a miracle from God to prove that Elijah's God was the true God.

Centuries later, in the 1200s, a group of European monks began to live on Mount Carmel. They honored Mary the Mother of God as Our Lady of Mount Carmel. For this reason the people began to call them friars of the Blessed Virgin Mary of Mount Carmel. This was the way the Carmelite order began. Pope Honorius III approved the order's rule in 1226. Simon Stock, an Englishman, became the superior of all the Carmelites in 1247. He helped the order expand and adapt to the times. He patterned the order on the Dominicans and Franciscans.

On July 16, 1251, Mary appeared to St. Simon and gave him the brown scapular. She promised her protection to all those who would wear the blessed habit. Many miracles proved her words. St. Pius X was pope from 1903 until 1914. He said that people could have the same blessings if they would wear the scapular medal. This medal has a picture of Our Lady of the Scapular on one side and the Sacred Heart on the other. Simon Stock died in Bordeaux, France, in 1265.

Let us wear the scapular or scapular medal. We will be protected by Our Lady in life and helped by her in death. And after death, she will bring us to heaven.

JULY 17

ST. LEO IV

St. Leo lived in the ninth century. He was a Roman by birth and spent his life in that city. Leo was educated in the Benedictine monastery near St. Peter's Basilica. He was ordained a priest and performed his ministry at St. John Lateran's, a large, famous basilica. Leo was well-known and loved by two popes, Gregory IV who died in 844, and Sergius II who died in 847. The death of Pope Sergius II was to have an immediate effect on Leo. Rumors of a barbarian invasion of Saracens had Romans terrified. They did not want to be left without a pope. Neither did the cardinals. They quickly elected the successor to Sergius II. He is known to history as Leo IV.

As pope, Leo had the city walls repaired. The walls had been damaged the previous year by a Saracen attack. He beautified churches and brought many relics to Rome. He started a renewal program for the clergy. In fact, in 853 he called a synod for all Roman priests. He passed forty-two rules which helped priests live more fervent, prayerful and joy-filled lives.

A few bishops caused Leo great suffering because of their lives. They confronted the pope openly and would not change their ways. No matter how much Pope Leo was insulted, he remained just, patient and humble. He never let his troubles get the best of him. Leo kept giving his time and energy for Jesus and his Church. He loved the beautiful prayers of the liturgy and encouraged liturgical chant and music.

People loved St. Leo. Even during his lifetime, he was considered a miracle worker. It is said that he was responsible for stopping the terrible fire in the English quarter of Rome.

Pope Leo IV continued serving the Church with cheerfulness right up to the end of his life. He died on July 17, 855.

Pope St. Leo IV lived during frightening times. He had many troubles and challenges. But he always kept calm and joyful. When we get upset, we can ask St. Leo IV to help us keep calm.

JULY 18

ST. FREDERICK

Frederick lived in ninth-century Utrecht, in the central part of the Netherlands. When he was ordained a priest, Bishop Ricfried put him in charge of instructing converts. Around 825, he was chosen to succeed Ricfried as bishop of Utrecht. Bishop Frederick became acquainted with the people of his diocese. He really cared about them. He gave high priority to missionary work too. In fact, he sent St. Odulf and other brave priests to areas where the people were still pagan. He wanted them to hear the Good News.

Because of his position as bishop, Frederick made a few enemies. The emperor's sons were very outspoken about their stepmother's immoral living. They asked Bishop Frederick to speak to Empress Judith. The bishop approached her gently but honestly. The empress did not take the advice well. She grew angry and was insulted.

Another challenge was the people who lived in the northern part of Frederick's diocese called Walcheren. St. Frederick sent priests to bring the people there the love of Jesus. Frederick knew the area was dangerous and unfriendly. He kept close to the priests whom he sent. He encouraged them and tried to help the people receive Christianity. But they were not ready to listen in any way. They resented the bishop's concern for them.

St. Frederick continued his care of the diocese with love and diligence. Then on July 18, 838, a tragedy happened. The bishop had just celebrated Mass. He was quietly making his thanksgiving when two men lunged at him with knives. A sentence from Psalm 116 came to mind. Slowly, the dying bishop prayed: "I walk before the Lord in the land of the living." A few minutes later he died.

Some say Empress Judith sent the hired killers because of her hatred for the bishop. Others think the guilty party was the people from Walcheren. The murderers were never caught and convicted. But Bishop Frederick is honored as a martyr and a saint.

When we stand up for what is right, we will have to pay a price. St. Frederick's example shows us the kind of courage saints are made of. We can ask him to give us some of his courage.

JULY 19

ST. MACRINA

St. Basil the Elder and St. Emmelia had ten children. They raised their family in Caesarea. Their first child, Macrina, was born around 330. Macrina was engaged when she was twelve. This was a custom of the time. But the young man died suddenly and Macrina told her parents she wished to remain unmarried.

Macrina was the big sister to nine brothers and sisters. Along with her parents and herself, three of her brothers are saints. St. Basil the Great (January 2), St. Peter of Sebaste and St. Gregory of Nyssa were all bishops. Macrina helped raise the children and they loved her. St. Peter of Sebaste remembers her especially with gratitude because she took loving care of him when he was a baby. Peter had been born the year his father died. The children grew up and St. Basil the Great found an estate for his mother and Macrina. It was like a convent and many women in the area came to live a spiritual life there.

After St. Emmelia died, Macrina continued to live the kind of life a nun would lead. She worked hard and gave away everything the family owned except what she really needed. Her brother Basil died in 379. She, too, became ill later that year. Her brother, St. Gregory of Nyssa, came home to visit her. He had been away for eight years. He found Macrina near death. Her frail body rested on two boards. His sister died within hours.

St. Gregory, the local bishop and two priests carried Macrina's coffin to the grave. The funeral procession was long and many people wept. St. Gregory wrote about Macrina and that is how the beauty of her life became known.

St. Macrina was kind and patient with her younger brothers and sisters. She was a wonderful big sister. She can give us the strength to be the same toward our family members if we ask her.

JULY 20

ST. JOSEPH BARSABBAS

Today's saint is named in the Bible's Acts of the Apostles. St. Peter wanted to replace Judas after Jesus' resurrection. Peter asked the community to suggest someone. He wanted a person who had been among the disciples from the time Jesus was baptized by John until the Lord's death and resurrection. The first Christians proposed two men, both of whom were qualified to be apostles. One was Joseph, called Barsabbas, and the other was Matthias. "One of these men must become a witness with us of Jesus' resurrection," Peter said.

The community prayed. "Lord," they said, "you are familiar with each of us here. Help us to know the person who should take the place of Judas." Then they "cast lots." The man selected was Matthias. He was added to the company of apostles. Not much is known of Matthias or Joseph Barsabbas. The early Church writer, Eusebius, considered Joseph one of the seventy-two disciples.

Soon the disciples spread out and went to other places. This was necessary to avoid persecution. It is believed that Joseph Barsabbas preached in many places. He spent his energy to spread the Good News. Little else is known. In fact, his death is not even recorded. But his love for the Church and his dedication whether he was chosen or not, are his gift to us.

St. Joseph Barsabbas focused on living an honest life. He was not interested in positions of power and esteem. That is easier said than practiced. The next time we feel upset because we did not receive the praise we felt we deserved, we can pray to St. Joseph Barsabbas. We can ask him to help us give generously, even when the "other person" is chosen.

JULY 21

ST. LAWRENCE OF BRINDISI

Caesar Rossi was born in Brindisi, Italy, in 1559. Brindisi was part of the Kingdom of Naples, Italy. Caesar took the name Lawrence when he became a Capuchin Franciscan at the age of sixteen. He was sent to the University of Padua to study theology. Lawrence surprised everyone by learning six languages also. His first language was Italian. But he could also speak French, German, Greek, Spanish, Syriac and Hebrew. St. Lawrence had a wonderful knowledge of the Bible, too.

After he was ordained a priest, he became a popular preacher. Because he could speak Hebrew, he worked for the conversion of the Jews living in Rome. Later, St. Lawrence was sent to establish his order in Austria. The emperor, Rudolph II, did not want them to come. But Lawrence's tender care for victims of a plague won Emperor Rudolph to his cause.

Next, the emperor asked Lawrence to persuade the German princes to fight the Turks. The Turks were trying to wipe out Christendom. Lawrence did convince the princes. However, the leaders insisted that he go with the army into battle to make the victory certain. When the soldiers saw how large the Turkish army was, they wanted to quit. So St. Lawrence himself rode in the lead. He was armed only with the crucifix. The Christian soldiers took heart and fought bravely. The Turks were completely defeated. St. Lawrence received the praise. But he never prided himself for success. He put his trust in God and gave him the glory.

In 1602, St. Lawrence became the master general of his order. He worked, preached and wrote to spread the Good News. He went on important peace missions to Munich, Germany, and Madrid, Spain. The rulers of those places listened to him and the missions were successful. But St. Lawrence was very sick. He had been tired out by the hard traveling and the strain of his tasks. He died on his birthday, July 22, in 1619. He was proclaimed a saint by Pope Leo XIII in 1881. He was honored as "apostolic doctor" by Pope John XXIII in 1959.

Prayer is the secret of success in life. We can ask St. Lawrence of Brindisi to help us set aside time each day for conversation with God.

JULY 22

ST. MARY MAGDALENE

Mary Magdalene was from Magdala near the Sea of Galilee. Some people identify her as a well-known sinner when she first saw Our Lord. It seems that she was very beautiful and very proud. But after she met Jesus, she felt great sorrow for her evil life. When Jesus went to supper at the home of a rich man named Simon, Mary came to weep at his feet. Then, with her long, beautiful hair, she wiped his feet dry and anointed them with expensive perfume. Some people were surprised that Jesus let such a sinner touch him. Our Lord knew why. He could see into Mary's heart. He said, "Many sins are forgiven her, because she has loved much." Then to Mary he said kindly, "Your faith has saved you. Go in peace."

From then on, with the other holy women, Mary humbly served Jesus and his apostles. When Our Lord was crucified, she was there at the foot of his cross. She stayed with the Blessed Mother and St. John, unafraid for herself. All she could think about was that her Lord was suffering. No wonder Jesus said of her: "She has loved much." After Jesus' body had been placed in the tomb, Mary went to anoint it with spices early Easter Sunday morning. She was shocked when she saw that the tomb was empty. Not finding the sacred body, she began to weep. Suddenly she saw someone she thought was the gardener. She asked him if he knew where the body of her beloved Master had been taken. Then the man spoke in a voice she knew so well: "Mary!" It was Jesus, standing right there in front of her. He was risen from the dead. And he had chosen to reveal himself first to her. The Gospels show Mary as being sent by the Lord himself to announce the Good News of the resurrection to Peter and the apostles. In the early centuries of the Church, Mary Magdalene's feast was celebrated with the Mass of an apostle.

We can ask St. Mary Magdalene to give us grateful hearts. We want to appreciate what Jesus has done for us because he loves us.

JULY 23

ST. BRIDGET OF SWEDEN

Bridget was born in Sweden in 1303. From the time she was a child, she was greatly devoted to the passion of Jesus. When she was only ten, she seemed to see Jesus on the cross and hear him say, "Look at me, my daughter." "Who has treated you like this?" cried little Bridget. "They who despise me and refuse my love for them," answered Jesus. From then on, Bridget tried to stop people from offending Jesus.

When she was fourteen, she married eighteen-year-old Ulf. Like Bridget, Ulf had set his heart on serving God. They had eight children, of whom one was St. Catherine of Sweden. Bridget and Ulf served the Swedish court. Bridget was the queen's personal maid. Bridget tried to help King Magnus and Queen Blanche lead better lives. For the most part, they did not listen to her.

All her life, Bridget had marvelous visions and received special messages from God. In obedience to them, she visited many rulers and important people in the Church. She explained humbly what God expected of them. After her husband died, Bridget put away her rich clothes. She lived as a poor nun. Later, she started the order of the Most Holy Savior, also known as Bridgettines. She still kept up her own busy life, traveling about doing good everywhere. And through all this activity, Jesus continued to reveal many secrets to her. These she received without the least bit of pride.

Shortly before she died, the saint went on a pilgrimage to the Holy Land. At the shrines there, she had visions of what Jesus had said and done in that place. All St. Bridget's revelations on the sufferings of Jesus were published after her death. St. Bridget died in Rome on July 23, 1373. She was proclaimed a saint by Pope Boniface IX in 1391.

St. Bridget of Sweden had a deep appreciation for Jesus' suffering and death on the cross. We can ask her to help us be sensitive and grateful followers of Jesus.

JULY 24

ST. BORIS AND ST. GLEB

These two brothers were born toward the end of the tenth century. They were sons of St. Vladimir of Kiev, the first Christian prince in Russia. Their father had had many wives before he became a Christian. Afterwards, he had lived as Jesus teaches us in the Gospel. Boris and Gleb were his sons by his Christian wife Anne. They were true Christians, too.

In an attempt to acquire more power when King Vladimir died, his oldest son planned to kill Boris and Gleb. Boris was warned as he was coming back with his soldiers from a battle against some wandering tribes. His men at once prepared to defend Boris from his older brother, but he would not permit it. "It is better for me to die alone," he said, "than to be the occasion of death to many." So he sent them away and sat down to wait. During the night, he thought about the martyrs who had been put to death by their own close relatives. He thought of how empty life becomes if we make the things of earth too important. What really counts, he thought, is good deeds, true love and true religion. When in the morning, his brother's hired murderers arrived and began striking him with spears, Boris did nothing but call down peace on them.

St. Gleb was killed soon after. The wicked older brother invited him to come to his palace for a friendly visit. As he was sailing down the river, Gleb's boat was boarded by fierce, armed men. He was terrified at first and begged them not to kill him. Yet he would not defend himself by fighting, not even when he saw that they were determined to kill him. Instead, St. Gleb quietly prepared himself to die. "I am being killed," he said, "and for what I do not know. But you know, Lord. And I know you said that for your name's sake brother would bring death to brother." Only a few years after their deaths, the people of Russia began going on pilgrimages to the tomb of the two brothers. Miracles took place. St. Boris and St. Gleb are called martyrs because they accepted death as Christ did, without defending themselves. They died in 1015. Pope Benedict XIII proclaimed them saints in 1724.

When someone hurts our feelings today, we can whisper a prayer to St. Boris and St. Gleb. They will help us be patient and forgiving.

JULY 25

ST. JAMES THE GREATER

James was a fisherman like his father Zebedee and his brother John. He was on his father's boat mending his nets when the Lord passed by. Jesus called each of them, James and John, to become fishers of men, to join him in spreading the Good News. Zebedee watched as his two sons left the boat to follow Jesus.

With St. Peter and St. John, James was a special companion of Jesus. With them James was permitted to see what the other apostles did not see. With them he watched as Jesus raised the daughter of Jairus to life. With them he was taken up the mountain to see Jesus shining like the sun, with his robes white as snow. This event is called Jesus' Transfiguration. On Holy Thursday, the night before he died, Jesus led the apostles into the garden of Gethsemane. Matthew's Gospel tells us he invited Peter, James and John to accompany him to a secluded area to pray. They watched as the Master's face became saddened with grief. Then drops of blood began to form on his brow. It was a very sad moment, but the apostles were exhausted. They fell asleep. Then St. James ran in fear when the enemies of Jesus took him away. And James was not near the foot of the cross on Good Friday. But the Lord met up with him on Easter Sunday evening in the upper room. The resurrected Jesus came through the locked door and said, "Peace be to you." St. James and the other apostles would find that peace after the Holy Spirit's coming on Pentecost.

St. James began his ministry as an impulsive, outspoken man. He asked Jesus bluntly for a seat of honor in his kingdom. He demanded that Jesus send fire down on the villages that did not receive the Lord. But he had great faith in Jesus. Eventually, James learned to become humble and gentle. And he did become "first" in a way he could never have imagined. He was given the honor of being the first apostle to die for Jesus. Chapter 12 of the Acts of the Apostles tells us that King Herod Agrippa had St. James put to death by the sword. As a martyr James gave the greatest witness of all.

We can ask St. James to help us recognize our weaknesses. He will obtain from Jesus the graces we need to improve.

ST. JOACHIM AND ST. ANNE

St. Anne and St. Joachim are the parents of the Blessed Virgin Mary. They spent their lives worshiping God and doing good. They had one great sorrow, however: God had not sent them any children. For years and years, Anne had begged the Lord to give her a child. She promised to consecrate the baby to him. When she was already old, God answered her prayer in a far better way than she could ever have dreamed. The child born to St. Joachim and St. Anne was the Immaculate Virgin Mary. This holiest of all women was to become the Mother of God. Anne took tender care of little Mary for a few years. Then she gave her to the service of God, as she had promised she would.

Mary went to live in the holy Temple of Jerusalem. St. Joachim and St. Anne continued their lives of prayer until God called them home to heaven. Christians have always been especially devoted to St. Anne. Many beautiful churches have been built in her honor. Perhaps one of the most famous is the Shrine of St. Anne de Beaupre in Canada. Great crowds go there all year around to ask St. Anne's help in their sufferings.

St. Anne and St. Joachim were the parents of Mary and the grandparents of Jesus. We can ask them to bring us closer to Jesus and Mary.

JULY 27

ST. PANTALEON

Pantaleon came from Nicomedia, near the Black Sea, in Asia. He lived in the fourth century. He was such a famous doctor that Emperor Galerius Maximian chose him for his personal doctor. There, at the wicked, pagan court, Pantaleon got into trouble. He was a Christian, but little by little, he let the bad example around him ruin him. He began to agree with the false wisdom praised by the pagans. At last, he committed the great sin of giving up his Christian faith entirely.

A holy priest named Hermolaos was deeply saddened to see the famous doctor desert Jesus. He went to him. With his wise, kind words, he made Pantaleon realize what a sin he had committed. Pantaleon listened to him and admitted that he had been very wrong. He detested his sin and joined the Church once more. To make up for what he had done, he greatly desired to suffer and die for Jesus. In the meantime, he imitated Our Lord's charity by taking care of poor sick people without any charge.

When Emperor Diocletian began his persecution, Pantaleon at once gave away everything he owned to the poor. Not long afterward, some jealous doctors accused him of being a Christian. He was given the choice of denying his religion or of being put to death. Pantaleon absolutely refused to say he was not a Christian and no torture could make him do it. There has been strong devotion in past ages to this saint. In the East he is called the "great martyr and wonder-worker."

We can ask St. Pantaleon to give us the strength to avoid companions who are leading bad lives. We can also ask him to strengthen us to avoid TV and radio programs, books and magazines that could threaten our faith in Jesus.

ST. BOTVID

Botvid was born in Sweden. He lived near the end of the eleventh century. The young man was brought up a pagan. But when he went to England, he became a Christian. Although he was not a priest, he felt a great desire to spread the Gospel message. He wanted to share Christianity with his own countrymen. He would be a lay missionary.

For this reason, St. Botvid returned to Sweden to work for the Lord there. But he was not even satisfied then. He wanted the Gospel to be preached in Finland, too. So he bought a Finnish slave and taught him the Catholic religion. Then he set the slave free to go back to his own country and catechize there. That man repaid the saint for his goodness by a terrible act of ingratitude. St. Botvid set out in a boat to take him across the Baltic sea to Finland. When they went ashore and the saint was asleep, the wicked slave killed Botvid and sailed away with the boat. When the saint did not return, friends searched for him until they found his body. He died in 1100.

St. Botvid is honored as a martyr of charity and as one of the apostles of Sweden.

Today we should show appreciation and gratitude to our parents and teachers. We need to let them know how much their care means.

ST. MARTHA

Martha was the sister of Mary and Lazarus. They lived in the little town of Bethany near Jerusalem. They were dear friends of Jesus, and he often came to visit them. In fact, the Gospel tells us: "Jesus loved Martha, and her sister Mary and Lazarus." It was St. Martha who lovingly served the Lord when he visited them. One day, she was preparing a meal for Jesus and his disciples. She realized that the task would be easier if her sister would help. She watched Mary sitting quietly at Jesus' feet, listening to him. "Lord, tell my sister to help me," Martha suggested. Jesus was very pleased with Martha's loving service. However, he wanted her to know that listening to God's Word and praying is even more important. So he said gently, "Martha, Martha, you are anxious about many things, but only one thing is necessary. Mary has chosen the better part."

St. Martha's great faith in Jesus was seen when her brother Lazarus died. As soon as she heard that Jesus was coming to Bethany, Martha went to meet him. She trusted Jesus and felt the freedom to say: "Lord, if you had been here, my brother would not have died." Then Jesus told her that Lazarus would rise. He said, "He who believes in me, even if he die, shall live. Do you believe this?" And Martha answered, "Yes, Lord, I believe that you are the Christ, the Son of God, who has come into the world." Jesus worked a great miracle and raised Lazarus from the dead!

Later, Jesus came again to have supper with Lazarus, Martha and Mary. St. Martha served them at table as always. This time, though, Martha had a much more loving attitude. She served with a joyful heart.

Sometimes we don't like to do certain chores. They seem heavy and unpleasant. At those times, we can ask St. Martha to give us a joyful attitude. We can ask her to show us that the littlest thing we do becomes beautiful when we do it for Jesus.

JULY 30

ST. PETER CHRYSOLOGUS

Peter was born in the small town of Imola, Italy. He lived in the fifth century. Bishop Cornelius of Imola educated him and ordained him a deacon. Even as a boy, Peter understood that a person is truly great only if he can control his passions and put on the spirit of Christ.

When the archbishop of Ravenna, Italy, died, Peter was appointed by Pope St. Leo the Great to succeed him. This was around 433. As a priest and bishop, St. Peter was effective. He worked hard to wipe out the paganism still practiced in his diocese. He helped his people grow in faith.

It was as a preacher that St. Peter became famous. Indeed, "Chrysologus" means "golden word." Yet his sermons or homilies were all short. He was afraid his audience would get bored. Besides that, these sermons were not especially unusual or beautiful. But St. Peter's message was more valuable than gold. He preached with such enthusiasm and fire that people listened to him breathlessly. In his sermons, St. Peter urged everyone to receive Jesus often in Holy Communion. He wanted people to realize that the Body of the Lord should be the daily food for their souls.

This good archbishop also worked for the unity of all the members of the Catholic Church. He tried to prevent people from getting confused about what Catholics believe. He also tried to keep peace. St. Peter Chrysologus died on December 2, 450, in his hometown of Imola, Italy. For his wonderful sermons, so rich in teaching, Pope Benedict XIII declared St. Peter to be a Doctor of the Church in 1729.

When we find it hard to pay attention at Mass, we can ask St. Peter Chrysologus to be near us. He will help us receive the sermon with loving hearts. He will also help us prepare our hearts for Holy Communion.

JULY 31

ST. IGNATIUS OF LOYOLA

This famous founder of the Jesuits was born in 1491. He was from a Spanish noble family. As a boy, he was sent to be a page at the royal court. There he lived on the desire to someday become a great soldier and marry a beautiful lady. Later, he did, indeed, win honor for his courage in the battle of Pamplona. However, a wound from a cannon ball forced him to spend months in bed at Loyola Castle. Ignatius asked for some books to read. He preferred stories of knights, but only biographies of Jesus and the saints were available. Having nothing else to do, he read them. Gradually, the books began to make an impression on him. His life began to change. He said to himself: "These were men and women like me, so why can't I do what they have done?" All the glory he had wanted before seemed worthless now. He began to imitate the saints in their prayers, penances and good works.

St. Ignatius had to suffer temptations and humiliations. Before he could begin his great work of starting the Society of Jesus, he had to go back to school. He had to study Latin grammar. The rest of the students were little boys and Ignatius was thirty-three. Yet Ignatius went to the class because he knew he would need this knowledge to help him in his ministry. With patience and even a laugh now and then, he took the boys' jeers and taunts. During this time, he tried to teach and encourage people to pray. For this he was suspected of heresy and put in jail for a while! But that was not going to stop Ignatius. "The whole city does not contain as many chains as I desire to wear for love of Jesus," he said. Ignatius was forty-three when he graduated from the University of Paris. With six other students, he professed religious vows in 1534. Ignatius and his companions who were not yet priests were ordained in 1539. They promised to work for God in whatever way the Holy Father thought best. In 1540 their order was officially recognized by the pope. Before Ignatius died, there were one thousand members of the Society of Jesus or "Jesuits." They were doing much good work teaching and preaching. Ignatius often prayed, "Give me only your love and your grace. With this I am rich enough, and I have no more to ask." St. Ignatius died in Rome, on July 31, 1556. Pope Gregory XV proclaimed him a saint in 1622.

St. Ignatius read biographies of Jesus and the saints. These books gave him a deeper awareness of Jesus, Mary and the Church. We, too, can choose books of lives of saints for the encouragement we need to be generous followers of Jesus.

august

ST. ALPHONSUS LIGUORI

Alphonsus was born near Naples, Italy, in 1732. He was a hard-working student. He received his degree in law and became a famous lawyer. A mistake he made in court convinced Alphonsus of what he had already thought: he should give up his law practice and become a priest. His father tried to persuade him not to do it. However, Alphonsus had made up his mind. He became a priest. His life was filled with activity. He preached and wrote books. He started a religious congregation called "Redemptorists." Alphonsus offered wise spiritual direction and brought peace to people through the sacrament of Reconciliation. He also wrote hymns, played the organ and painted pictures.

St. Alphonsus wrote sixty books. This is incredible considering his many other responsibilities. He also was often sick. He had frequent headaches, but would hold something cold against his forehead and keep doing his work.

Although he was naturally inclined to be hasty, Alphonsus tried to control himself. He became so humble that when Pope Pius VI wanted to make him a bishop in 1798, he gently said "no." When the pope's messengers had come in person to tell him of the pope's choice, they called Alphonsus "Most illustrious Lord." Alphonsus said, "Please don't call me that again. It would kill me." The pope helped Alphonsus understand that he really wanted him to be a bishop. Alphonsus sent many preachers all over his diocese. The people needed to be reminded again of the love of God and the importance of their religion. Alphonsus told the priests to preach simple sermons. "I never preached a sermon that the simplest old woman in the church could not understand," he said.

As he got older, St. Alphonsus suffered from illnesses. He had painful arthritis and became crippled. He grew deaf and almost blind. He also had disappointments and temptations. But he had great devotion to the Blessed Mother as we know from his famous book called the *Glories of Mary.* The trials were followed by great peace and joy and a holy death.

Alphonsus died in 1787 at the age of ninety-one. Pope Gregory XVI proclaimed him a saint in 1839. Pope Pius IX proclaimed him a Doctor of the Church in 1871.

Let us increase our devotion to the Blessed Mother. We can ask St. Alphonsus to help us love Mary as he did.

ST. EUSEBIUS

Eusebius was born on the island of Sardinia, Italy, around 283. His parents were dedicated Christians. It is believed that his father died a martyr. Eusebius was always active in the Christian community. He was called to serve the people of Rome and then went to northern Italy, to Vercelli. He was chosen to be the first bishop of Vercelli. He and some of his priests lived a common life modeled on a monastery. The priests received wonderful preparation for growing in the spiritual life. They also learned how to direct other people who would come to them for guidance. The priests trained by St. Eusebius became fervent and happy ministers of Jesus. Many were ordained bishops.

During this time, the Arian heresy was widespread. Many people were confused about it and believed it to be true. Emperor Constantius was an Arian, too, and he wanted to win everybody to his side. Bishops who would not give in were sent away from their diocese. St. Athanasius was condemned in 355. Eusebius was at the Council of Milan that condemned him. But Eusebius would not cast his vote against Athanasius, so he was banished too. Eusebius was exiled to Palestine. At first, a kind man kept him as a respected guest in his house. But then the man died and the Arians kidnapped the bishop. They insulted him, dragged him through the streets and kept him in a small room for four days. Then when representatives from the diocese of Vercelli demanded that he be released and returned to his former lodging, he was. But a short time later, the bishop was beaten and harassed again. When Constantius died in 361, the next emperor permitted the exiled bishops to return to their own dioceses.

St. Eusebius was a champion of truth. Other great bishops of that time were too, such as St. Athanasius and St. Meletius. It is believed that St. Eusebius is one of the persons who contributed to the preparation of the "Athanasian Creed." This is one of the precious creeds that states what we as Catholics believe. He spent the rest of his years in Vercelli among the people of his diocese. Bishop Eusebius died on August 1, 371.

From St. Eusebius we can learn that our faith is a great treasure. Like him, we should love and appreciate it. We might want to ask ourselves: Am I willing to sacrifice for what I believe? It means being willing to make upright choices: avoiding movies, videos and songs that are not sensitive to Christian values.

ST. PETER JULIAN EYMARD

In 1811, Peter was born in a small town in the diocese of Grenoble, France. He worked with his father making and repairing knives until he was eighteen. Peter spent his free hours studying. He taught himself Latin and received instruction in the faith from a helpful priest. In the back of Peter's mind was a longing to become a priest. When he was twenty, he began his studies at the seminary of Grenoble. Peter Julian became a priest in 1834 and served in two parishes during the next five years. The people realized what a gift he was to them. When Father Eymard asked his bishop's permission to join a new religious order called the Marists, the bishop gave his consent. Father Eymard served the Marists as spiritual director of the seminarians. In 1845, he became the superior of Lyons, France. But even though Father Eymard fulfilled many diligent responsibilities all his life, he is remembered especially for something else.

Father Eymard had a glowing love for the Holy Eucharist. He was very attracted to the presence of Jesus in the Eucharist. He loved to spend time daily in adoration. One feast of Corpus Christi (the feast of the Body and Blood of Jesus), Father Eymard had a powerful religious experience. As he carried the sacred Host in procession, he felt the presence of Jesus like warmth from a fireplace. The

Host seemed to surround him with love and light. In his heart, he spoke to the Lord about the spiritual and material needs of all people. He begged that the mercy and love of Jesus touch everyone as he had been touched through the Eucharist.

In 1856, Father Eymard followed an inspiration that he had prayed about for several years. With the approval of his superiors, he started a religious order of priest-adorers of the Holy Eucharist. They became known as the Priests of the Blessed Sacrament. Two years after the order of priests was begun, Father Eymard began an order of sisters, the Servants of the Blessed Sacrament. Like the priests, these sisters had a special love for Jesus in the Holy Eucharist. They devoted their lives to adoration of Jesus. Father Eymard started parish organizations to help people be prepared to receive First Communion. He wrote several books on the Eucharist that were translated into different languages. The books are still available in English today.

Father Eymard lived at the same time in history as the saint we celebrate tomorrow, August 4—St. John Vianney. The two men were friends and each highly admired the other. Father Vianney said that Father Eymard was a saint and added, "Adoration by priests! How fine! I will pray for Father Eymard's work every day."

St. Peter Julian Eymard spent the last four years of his life in severe pain. He also suffered because of difficulties and criticism. But Father Eymard continued his life of adoring the Eucharist. His witness and his sacrifice helped many others find

their call in his religious orders. He died on August 1, 1868, at the age of fifty-seven. Pope John XXIII proclaimed him a saint on December 9, 1962.

We can ask St. Peter Julian Eymard to give us some of his love for Jesus in the Holy Eucharist. We can ask him to help us learn from him how to adore the Holy Eucharist.

AUGUST 4

ST. JOHN VIANNEY

John Mary Vianney was born in Lyons, France, in 1786. As a child he took care of his father's sheep. He loved to pray but he also loved to play horseshoes. When John was eighteen, he asked his father's permission to become a priest. His father was worried because John had become a big help on the family farm. After two years, Mr. Vianney agreed. At twenty, John studied under Father Balley. The priest was very patient but Latin soon became a major problem for John. He became discouraged. It was then that he decided to walk sixty miles to the shrine of St. John Francis Regis, a popular saint in France. We celebrate his feast on June 16. John prayed for help. After that pilgrimage, he had as much trouble as ever with his studies. The difference was that he never again grew discouraged.

John was finally able to enter the seminary. Studies were hard. No matter how much he tried, he never did very well. When the final examinations came, they were spoken, not written. John had to face a board of teachers and answer their questions. He was so upset that he broke down in the middle of the test. Yet, because John was a holy man, he was full of common sense and he understood what the Church taught about the subjects. He knew the right answers when asked what should be done in this case or that. He just couldn't say those answers in the complicated style of Latin text books. John was ordained anyway. He understood what the priestly vocation was and his goodness was beyond question.

He was sent to a little parish called Ars. Father Vianney fasted and did hard penance for his people. He tried to stop them from sinning. They drank too much, worked all day Sunday and never went to church. Many used terrible language. Eventually, one tavern after another closed down because business became so slow. People began to worship regularly on Sundays and attended weekday Mass. The swearing was not so frequent. What had happened in Ars? "Our priest is a saint," the people would say, "and we must obey him."

God gave John the power to see into people's minds and to know the future. Because of this gift, he converted many sinners and helped people make the right decisions. Pilgrims began to come to Ars. In time, it was hundreds a day. St. John Vianney spent twelve to sixteen hours daily hearing confessions. He wanted so much to spend the rest of his life in a monastery. Instead, he stayed forty-two years at Ars and died there in 1859 at the age of seventy-three. St. John Vianney was proclaimed a saint in 1925 by Pope Pius XI.

St. John Vianney teaches us by his example to pray when things are hard. The Lord will help us overcome our difficulties. He will use us as his instruments to bring his love and joy.

AUGUST 5

BLESSED FREDERIC JANSSOONE

Blessed Frederic Janssoone was born in Flanders in 1838. His life took many interesting turns. His was not an ordinary nineteenth-century way of life. Frederic was born of wealthy farm parents and he was the youngest of thirteen children. He was just nine when his father died, so the boy left school to help support his mother. He soon realized that he had a "knack" for selling. He enjoyed people. He liked meeting new people and he knew how to explain his products.

Frederic's mother died in 1861. It was then that the twenty-three-year-old reached into his heart in search of his own life's call. He realized that he was experiencing a strong desire to join the Franciscan order. After his seminary studies were finished, Frederic was ordained a Franciscan priest. He became a military chaplain for a time. Then in 1876, he was sent to the Holy Land. Father Frederic preached the Gospel in the places made sacred by Jesus himself.

He used his skills to help various groups of Christians cooperate in the upkeep of two sacred churches. He built a church in Bethlehem. Blessed Frederic is also remembered for reviving an old custom of having pilgrims make the Stations of the Cross throughout the streets of Jerusalem.

Father Frederic's ministry in Canada began when he was transferred there in 1881. He was sent on a fundraising tour. His many talents served him well. His joyful spirit of self-giving made him much loved immediately. His sermons and talks were filled with interesting facts about the Holy Land. He looked into the faces and hearts of the people and prayed that they would grow in the richness of God's life. In 1888, he returned to Canada to stay and was to spend the rest of his life there.

Father Janssoone was an interesting person and a fascinating writer. He wrote several articles and biographies of saints. They are reminders of the enthusiasm that filled his own soul. They reflect the joy of Jesus that he so willingly shared with others. Father Frederic died on August 4, 1916. He was declared "blessed" in 1988 by Pope John Paul II.

We can learn from Blessed Frederic Janssoone how to be joyful givers and happy followers of Jesus. We can use our gifts to spread joy and to be images of Jesus, the way Blessed Frederic did.

AUGUST 6

THE TRANSFIGURATION

The Gospels of Matthew, Mark and Luke record the marvelous event of the Lord's Transfiguration. Before he suffered and died, he let three of his apostles see him shining with great glory. He did this to make their belief in him stronger.

Jesus took Peter, James and John with him up Mount Tabor which stands in the middle of Galilee. When they were by themselves, suddenly the Lord's face began to shine bright like the sun. His robes became white as snow. The apostles were speechless. As they watched, two famous prophets of old, Elijah and Moses, appeared. They were talking with Jesus. Imagine the joy those apostles felt. "Lord," said St. Peter, "it is good for us to be here. If you want, let us set up three tents here— one for you, one for Moses, and one for Elijah." Peter really did not know what to say, because he was trembling with wonder and fear. As he was talking, a bright cloud overshadowed them. From it the voice of God the Father came, saying, "This is my beloved Son; hear him."

When they heard that, the apostles were so struck with fear that they fell on their faces. Then Jesus came near and touched them. "Arise," he said. "Do not be afraid." When they looked up, they saw no one but Jesus. As they came down the mountain, Jesus told them not to tell anyone what they had seen until he had risen from the dead. They did not understand what he meant by these words then. But after his glorious resurrection on Easter Sunday, they would realize what Jesus had meant.

Let us listen to what Jesus tells us through his vicar, the pope, and through our bishops and priests.

AUGUST 7

The current Roman calendar lists two saints on August 7. Their stories are briefly presented here one after the other.

ST. SIXTUS II AND COMPANIONS

The Roman emperors who persecuted Christians were trying to wipe out belief in Jesus and a religion they hated and feared. Although they did not know it, every time they murdered a saint, they gave Christians one more reason for belief. From the bloody Roman persecutions came the martyrs. The martyrs' gift of faithfulness to Jesus, even at the cost of their lives, will bless the Church until the end of time.

The persecution of Emperor Valerian caused the martyrdom of Pope St. Sixtus II and six deacons in one day. The persecution was fierce. Many in the Christian community gathered in the underground catacombs. They participated in the Mass and encouraged each other. Sixtus, a priest of Rome, became pope in 257. That same year Valerian's persecution began. Sixtus carried on bravely for a year, mostly from hiding, encouraging the Christians. With tact and gentleness, he even settled issues about Christian beliefs. Then on August 6, 258, Roman soldiers broke into a room in the catacombs as Sixtus sat peacefully. He was preaching a sermon about Jesus' love and forgiveness. Some say he was killed right there in his chair, along with four of the six deacons. Others say he and the deacons were taken away for trial. Then they were brought back to that very room, where they were killed. The two remaining deacons were killed later in the day.

A century later, Pope St. Damasus wrote a beautiful inscription on the tomb of St. Sixtus which is in the catacombs of St. Callistus in Rome. St. Sixtus II was so highly thought of by the early Christians that he is among the saints listed in the Church's First Eucharistic Prayer of the Mass.

We can ask St. Sixtus II to help us appreciate our gift of faith and grow in our love for Jesus. When we are afraid to stand up for what Jesus expects of us, we can pray to St. Sixtus and his companion martyrs for courage.

ST. CAJETAN

Cajetan was born in Vicenza, Italy, in 1480, the son of a count. He graduated from the University of Padua with law degrees. Then he worked in the papal offices in Rome. Cajetan became a priest in 1516. He returned to his own city of Vicenza. Although it angered his rich relatives, the saint joined a group of humble, simple men who devoted themselves to helping the sick and the poor. St. Cajetan would go all over the city looking for unfortunate people and would serve them himself. He helped at the hospital by caring for people with the most disgusting diseases. In other cities, he did the same charitable work. He also kept encouraging everyone to go to Holy Communion often. "I shall never be happy," he said, "until I see Christians flocking to feed on the Bread of Life with eagerness and delight, not with fear and shame."

Together with three other holy men, St. Cajetan started an order of religious priests called "Theatines." This group devoted themselves to preaching. They encouraged frequent confession and Communion, helping the sick and other good works.

Cajetan died at the age of sixty-seven. In his last sickness, he lay on hard boards, even though the doctor advised him to have a mattress. "My Savior died on a cross," he said. "Let me at least die on wood." Cajetan passed away on August 7, 1547, in Naples. He was proclaimed a saint by Pope Clement X in 1671.

In imitation of this saint, we should make the Holy Eucharist the center of our lives. We can ask St. Cajetan to help us love the Eucharist as he did.

AUGUST 8

ST. DOMINIC

Dominic was born in Castile, Spain, in 1170. He was a member of the Guzman family and his mother is Blessed Joan of Aza. When Dominic was seven, he began to go to school. His uncle, a priest, directed his education. After years of study, he became a priest too. Dominic lived a quiet life of prayer and obedience with other virtuous priests. But God had amazing plans for Dominic. He was meant to begin a new religious order. It would be called the Order of Preachers or "Dominicans," after St. Dominic.

The Dominicans preached the faith. They helped correct false teachings called heresies. It all began when Dominic was on a trip through southern France. He realized that the heresy of Albigensianism was doing great harm. St. Dominic felt such pity for the people who had joined it. He wanted to help them. The Dominicans conquered that dangerous heresy with prayer, especially the Holy Rosary. Dominic also encouraged the people to be humble and to make sacrifices. Once someone asked St. Dominic what book he used to prepare his wonderful sermons. "The only book I use is the book of love," he said. He always prayed to be filled with true love of neighbor. He urged the Dominicans to be devoted to the study of the Bible and to prayer. No one did more than St. Dominic and his preachers to spread the beautiful practice of saying the Rosary.

St. Dominic was a brilliant preacher, while St. Francis of Assisi was a humble beggar. Yet, they were close friends. Their two orders of Dominicans and Franciscans helped Christians become holier. Dominic's friars opened centers in Paris, France; Madrid, Spain; Rome and Bologna, Italy. He lived to see his order spread to Poland, Scandinavia and Palestine. The friars also went to Canterbury, London, and Oxford, England. Dominic died in Bologna on August 7, 1221. His great friend, Cardinal Ugolino of Venice became Pope Gregory IX. He proclaimed Dominic a saint in 1234.

We can ask St. Dominic to help us grow in our love for our Catholic faith. We can also ask him to teach us how to be as devoted to the Rosary as he was.

AUGUST 9

BLESSED JOHN OF RIETI

Blessed John lived in the first half of the fourteenth century. He has a sister who is also "blessed," Blessed Lucy of Amelia. They were members of the Bufalari family from the Umbria region of Italy. John felt a call to religious life. He was attracted to the order of St. Augustine and wanted to be a brother. John was accepted into the order and found himself immediately at home. He loved to pray and to meditate about Jesus, Mary and the saints. He learned how to talk to God, his Father, and he especially took the opportunities to serve at Mass. People from the neighboring towns came to Mass at the church of the Augustinians. They noticed the brother who was always there. He was so peaceful and kind. Brother John went out of his way to welcome them. He made them feel at home.

When people came to the monastery in need, Brother John was there to greet and welcome them. For those who were staying overnight, he would bring them to the guest rooms and wait on them. He would make sure they had food, medicine and whatever else the monastery could give.

The years passed. Brother John continued his religious life with the quiet rhythm of a clock. He was steady and stable. Blessed John remained joyful in his vocation until his death in 1350. It was no surprise to anybody who had come to the monastery when miracles started to be reported at his tomb. Brother John was not going to let his death stop him from performing his ministry for Jesus.

Fun and excitement will not keep us happy for very long. What really fills us with happiness is what is inside of us—our faith and love for Jesus. We can ask Blessed John to help us find the happiness he found.

AUGUST 10

ST. LAWRENCE

This famous martyr of Rome lived in the third century. He was one of seven deacons who were in charge of giving help to the poor and the needy. When a persecution broke out, Pope St. Sixtus II was condemned to death. As he was led to execution, Lawrence followed him weeping. "Father, where are you going without your deacon?" "I am not leaving you, my son," answered the pope. "In three days you will follow me." Full of joy, Lawrence gave to the poor the rest of the money he had on hand. He even sold expensive church vessels to have more to give away.

The prefect of Rome, a greedy man, thought the Church had a great fortune hidden away. He ordered Lawrence to bring the Church's treasure to him. The saint said he would, in three days. Then he went through the city and gathered together all the poor and sick people supported by the Church. He showed them to the prefect and said: "This is the Church's treasure." The prefect was furious. In his anger he condemned Lawrence to a slow, cruel death. The saint was tied on top of an iron grill over a slow fire that roasted him. God gave him so much strength and joy that Lawrence is said to have joked. "Turn me over," he said to the judge. Before he died, he prayed that the city of Rome might be converted to Jesus. He prayed that the Catholic faith would spread all over the world.

Lawrence died on August 10, 158. His feast spread throughout Italy and northern Africa. Emperor Constantine built a beautiful basilica in Lawrence's honor. St. Lawrence is among the saints mentioned in the First Eucharistic Prayer at Mass.

When we feel like complaining about something that bothers us, we can whisper a prayer to St. Lawrence. We can ask him to help us be patient.

ST. CLARE

Clare was born around 1193 in Assisi, Italy. She lived at the time of St. Francis of Assisi. Clare became the foundress of an order of nuns called the "Poor Clares." When she was eighteen, she heard St. Francis preach. Her heart burned with a great desire to imitate him. She also wanted to live a poor, humble life for Jesus. So one evening, she ran away from home. In a little chapel outside Assisi, she gave herself to God. St. Francis cut off her hair and offered her a rough brown habit to wear. She stayed with the Benedictine nuns until more nuns would join her. Her parents tried in every way to make her return home, but Clare would not. Soon her fifteen-year-old sister Agnes joined her. Other young women wanted to be brides of Jesus, too. Before long there was a small religious community.

St. Clare and her nuns wore no shoes. They never ate meat. They lived in a poor house and kept silent most of the time. Yet they were very happy because they felt that Jesus was close to them. Once an army of rough soldiers came to attack Assisi. They planned to raid the convent first. Although very sick, St. Clare asked to be carried to the wall. She had the Blessed Sacrament placed right where the soldiers could see it. Then she knelt and begged God to save the nuns. "O

Lord, protect these sisters whom I cannot protect now," she prayed. And a voice within her seemed to say: "I will keep them always in my care." At the same time, a sudden fright struck the attackers. They fled as fast as they could.

St. Clare was abbess of her convent for forty years. Twenty-nine of those years she was sick. But she said that she was joyful anyway because she was serving the Lord. Some people worried that the nuns were suffering because they were so poor. "They say that we are too poor, but can a heart which possesses the infinite God be truly poor?" St. Clare died on August 11, 1253. Just two years later she was proclaimed a saint by Pope Alexander IV.

Sometimes we forget to give enough time to the Lord. We might be so excited about certain things that we drown out the voice of Jesus. That is when we can ask St. Clare to show us how to keep in touch with Jesus who lives in our hearts.

AUGUST 12

ST. PORCARIUS AND COMPANIONS

In the fifth century, a large abbey for monks was built off the coast of Provence, which is southern France today. It was called the abbey of Lerins. The abbey was filled with many holy monks. By the eighth century, the community of Lerins was made up of monks, novices, students and young men interested in becoming monks. There were over five hundred men.

Around 732, Abbot Porcarius had some kind of a revelation or premonition. The monastery was about to be attacked by barbarian invaders. Abbot Porcarius packed all the students and thirty-six of the younger monks onto a boat. He sent them off to safety. Because there were no more boats, he gathered the remainder of the community around him. Nobody complained about being left behind. Instead, they prayed together for courage. They asked the Lord for the gift to forgive their enemies.

Soon Saracens from Spain or North Africa landed their ships. They attacked the monks, just as the abbot had predicted. The monks prayed and encouraged one another to bravely suffer and die for Christ. The attackers pounced on their prey and killed all but four who were carried off as slaves. St. Porcarius and the monks of Lerins had become brave martyrs for Jesus.

We can pray every day for those who persecute Jesus and his Church. We can also ask St. Porcarius and the monks of Lerins to inspire all people to value and protect human life from the moment of conception until death.

AUGUST 13

ST. PONTIAN AND ST. HIPPOLYTUS

A man named Maximinus became the emperor of Rome in 235. Almost immediately, he began a persecution of the Christians. One of the frequent punishments of bishops and priests was to be sent into exile to the dangerous and unhealthy mine fields in Sardinia, Italy. It was this very persecution that joined the two martyrs celebrated today.

St. Pontian became pope after the death of Urban I in the year 230. When Maximinus became emperor, Pontian served the Church with his sufferings in the mines of Sardinia.

The other saint on today's calendar is St. Hippolytus. He was a priest and a scholar in the church of Rome. He wrote many excellent works of theology and was a great teacher. Hippolytus had become frustrated with Pope St. Zephyrinus, who had been martyred in the year 217. Hippolytus felt that the pope had not been quick enough to stop people who were teaching errors. St. Zephyrinus' successor had been St. Callistus I. Hippolytus had not been pleased with the choice of the new pope. Hippolytus himself had a large following, and he gave in to their suggestion that he be appointed pope. So he agreed. He broke ties with the Church and became a false pope. When the persecution began, he was arrested and sent to Sardinia. There in that sad environment, while the

97

enemies of Christianity laughed, a miracle of healing took place.

Pope Pontian and Hippolytus met in exile. The priest was touched by the humility of the pope. He asked to return to the Church and felt the anger lifted from his heart. Pope Pontian understood the priest and loved him. He realized their need to help and encourage each other in their love for Jesus. Both became martyrs and remain for all time witnesses of forgiveness and Christian hope.

If we should ever become angry and frustrated about something, we have these two saints to help us. We can ask St. Pontian for his understanding heart and St. Hippolytus for his loving obedience.

AUGUST 14

ST. MAXIMILIAN KOLBE

Raymond Kolbe was born in Poland in 1894. He joined the Franciscan order in 1907 and took the name that we know him by: Maximilian. Maximilian loved his vocation very much, and he especially loved the Blessed Mother. He added the name "Mary" when he pronounced solemn vows in 1914. Father Maximilian Mary was convinced that the world of the twentieth century needed their Heavenly Mother to guide and protect them. He used the press to make Mary more widely known. He and his fellow Franciscans published two monthly newsletters that soon went to readers around the world.

The Mother of God blessed Father Maximilian's work. He built a large center in Poland. This center was called "City of the Immaculate." By 1938, eight hundred Franciscans lived there and labored to make the love of Mary known. Father Kolbe also started another City of the Immaculate in Nagasaki, Japan. Still another was begun in India. In 1938, the Nazis invaded the Polish City of the Immaculate. They stopped the wonderful work going on there. In 1941, the Nazis arrested Father Kolbe. They sentenced him to hard manual labor at Auschwitz. He was at Auschwitz three months when a prisoner successfully escaped. The Nazis made the rest of the prisoners pay for the escape. They chose ten prisoners at random to die in the starvation bunker. All the prisoners stood at attention, while ten men were pulled out of line. One chosen prisoner, a married man with a family, begged and pleaded to be spared for the sake of his children. Father Kolbe, who had not been picked, listened and felt deeply moved to help that suffering prisoner. He stepped forward and asked the commander if he could take the man's place. The commander accepted his offer.

Father Kolbe and the other prisoners were marched into the starvation bunker. They remained alive without food or water for several days. One by one, as they died, Father Kolbe helped and comforted them. He was the last to die. An injection of carbolic acid hastened his death on

August 14, 1941. Pope John Paul II proclaimed him a saint and a martyr in 1982.

St. Maximilian Mary Kolbe is the kind of person we all want to be. He was a hero who gave up his life that someone else might live. He was such a special person because he was a great friend of the Blessed Mother. We can be friends of Mary, too, if we honor her and pray to her.

AUGUST 15

THE ASSUMPTION OF THE BLESSED VIRGIN MARY

This feast of Mary celebrates a special privilege of Mary, our Mother. The Assumption means that she entered into the glory of heaven not only with her soul, but also with her body. The Son of God took his body from Mary's pure womb. It was fitting, then, that her body should be glorified as soon as her life here on earth was ended.

Now Mary is in heaven. She is queen of heaven and earth. She is the Mother of Jesus' Church and queen of apostles. Every time Mary asks Jesus to give us graces, he listens to her request.

After the resurrection from the dead, we, too, can go to heaven with our bodies. If we use our bodies now to do good, those bodies will share in our heavenly reward.

After the resurrection, our bodies will be perfect. They will not be subject to illness anymore. They will not need any more food and drink to keep alive. They will be able to go every place without time or effort. They will be beautiful and splendid!

Mary's Assumption body and soul into heaven is a dogma of faith. This wonderful truth was proclaimed by Pope Pius XII on November 1, 1950.

It is so wonderful to be able to think that we have a special Mother in heaven. She really does love us. She is there for us whenever we call to her in prayer. We can whisper a Hail Mary often throughout the day.

AUGUST 16

ST. STEPHEN OF HUNGARY

St. Stephen was born around 969 in Hungary. This saint's name had been Vaik. When he became a Christian at the age of ten, he was given the name of Stephen. At the same time, his father, the duke of Hungary, and many nobles also became Christians. However, when Stephen himself became king, the country was still quite pagan. Some people were violent and fierce. So he decided to establish the Church solidly in Hungary. His efforts were blessed by God. The secret of St. Stephen's amazing success in leading his people to the Christian faith was his devotion to Mary. He placed his whole kingdom under her protection and built a magnificent church in her honor.

Pope Sylvester II sent a beautiful king's crown to Stephen. This treasure became known as the crown of St. Stephen. During the Second World War, American soldiers captured the crown. However, it was returned to Hungary in 1978.

Stephen was a strong, fearless ruler. He enforced just laws. But he was also gentle and kind to the poor. He tried to avoid war as much as he could. He loved to give gifts of money to beggars without letting them know who he was. Once he was giving these gifts in disguise when a crowd of rough beggars knocked him down and struck him. They pulled his hair and beard, and stole his money pouch. They never could have imagined they were bullying their king. And they never found out from him. He took the insult quietly and humbly. He forced his thoughts to turn to Mary and prayed: "See, Queen of heaven, how your people have treated him whom you made king. If they were enemies of the faith, I would know what to do with them. But since they are your Son's subjects, I will take this joyfully. I say thank you for it." In fact, King Stephen made a promise then and there to give more than ever to beggars.

Stephen was king of Hungary for forty-two years. He died on August 15, 1038. St. Stephen was proclaimed a saint by Pope St. Gregory VII in 1083.

We don't have to be kings or presidents to realize the powerful impact of example. Some people preach wonderful sermons every day by the way they live. When we need more courage to imitate the good example of people, we can ask St. Stephen of Hungary to help us.

BLESSED JOAN DELANOUE

The youngest of twelve children, Joan Delanoue was born in 1666. Her family had a small but successful business. When her widowed mother died, she left the store to Joan. She was not an evil girl, but she thought only of making money. She committed many little sins to do it. She had once been devout, but now there was little love in her heart. Her mother had always been generous to beggars. Joan, instead, would buy food only just in time for dinner. This way she could tell any beggars who came to the door during the day: "I have nothing to give you."

Joan was not happy living like this. At last, when she was twenty-seven, a good priest helped her start living up to her faith with love and fervor. Then she finally saw that her "business" was to give away money, not hoard it. Joan began taking care of poor families and orphans. Eventually, she closed her shop entirely to devote her time to them. People called her house full of orphans, "Providence House." Later, she persuaded other young women to help her. They became the Sisters of St. Anne of Providence in Saumur, France, Joan's town.

Joan lived a very self-sacrificing life. She performed hard penances. St. Grignon de Montfort met Joan. He thought at first that her pride was causing her to be so hard on herself. But then he realized that her heart was really full of love of God. He said: "Go on in the way you have begun. God's Spirit is with you. Follow his voice and fear no more." Joan died peacefully on August 17, 1736. She was seventy years old. The people of Saumur said, "That little shopkeeper did more for the poor of Saumur than all the town councilors put together. What a woman! And what a holy person!" Joan was proclaimed "blessed" by Pope Pius XII in 1947, the same year St. Grignon de Montfort was declared a saint.

Many people die every day of hunger. We can realize the importance of not wasting food. Even if something is put on our plate that we don't like, we can eat it. We can ask Blessed Joan to give us her self-sacrificing spirit.

ST. JANE FRANCES DE CHANTAL

Jane was born in Dijon, France, in 1572. Her father was a devout man. He brought up his children well after the death of his wife. Jane, whom he dearly loved, married Christopher, the baron de Chantal. Jane and Christopher loved each other very much. God blessed them with six children, four of whom lived. Jane showed her love for God by loving her husband and children with her whole heart. Then, suddenly, a great sorrow fell upon that happy home. Baron Christopher was accidentally shot by a friend who had gone hunting with him. When he died, Jane was heart-broken. She forgave the man who had caused his death and even became his child's godmother.

St. Jane began to ask the Lord to send a holy priest into her life for guidance. In the meantime, she prayed and brought up her children in the love of God. She visited the poor and the sick and comforted the dying. When she met St. Francis de Sales, she knew this was the holy man God had sent to guide her. We celebrate his feast on January 24. Following his plan, Jane and three other young women started the order of the Visitation. But first, she had to make sure that her children, although older, were settled. She had other responsibilities and challenges too. But Jane tried to follow God's plan as she saw it, no matter how difficult.

St. Jane was courageous in all the difficulties she faced. She opened up many convents and struggled as well with her own temptations. She seems to have struggled with doubts. "Despite all her suffering," wrote St. Vincent de Paul, "her face never lost its peaceful look. And she was always faithful to God. So I consider her one of the holiest souls I have ever met."

St. Jane died on December 13, 1641. She was proclaimed a saint by Pope Clement XIII in 1767.

Like St. Jane, we too can be true to God's plan for us, even when we have to make sacrifices. We can ask St. Jane for some of her courage and will power.

AUGUST 19

ST. JOHN EUDES

John Eudes was born in Normandy, France, in 1601. He was the oldest son of a farmer. Even as a child, he tried to copy the example of Jesus in the way he treated his family, friends and neighbors. When he was only nine, another boy slapped his face. John felt himself becoming angry. Then he remembered Jesus' words in the Gospel: to turn the other cheek. So he did.

John's parents wanted him to marry and have a family. He gently but firmly convinced them that he had a priestly call. He joined the congregation of the Oratory and studied for the priesthood. After

John was a priest, the plague hit Normandy. It brought terrible suffering and death. Father Eudes volunteered to help the sick, caring for both their souls and bodies. Later, he became a popular preacher of missions in parishes. In fact, during his lifetime he preached 110 missions. St. John is responsible for the establishment of important religious congregations: the Sisters of Our Lady of Charity and the Good Shepherd nuns. Father Eudes also started the Congregation of Jesus and Mary for priests. This congregation was dedicated to training young men to become good parish priests.

St. John was very devoted to the Sacred Heart of Jesus and to the Holy Heart of Mary. He wrote a book about these devotions. John became sick after he preached an outdoor mission in very cold weather. He never fully recovered. John died in 1680. He was proclaimed "blessed" by Pope St. Pius X in 1908. This pope called John Eudes the apostle of devotions to the Sacred Heart of Jesus and the Immaculate Heart of Mary. He was proclaimed a saint by Pope Pius XI in 1925.

We can ask St. John Eudes to show us how to grow in love of the Sacred Hearts of Jesus and Mary. We can also find out about devotion to the Nine First Fridays and the Five First Saturdays so that we can practice them.

AUGUST 20

ST. BERNARD

Bernard was born in 1090 in Dijon, France. He and his six brothers and sisters received an excellent education. His heart was broken when his mother died. He was just seventeen. He might have let sadness get the best of him had it not been for his lively sister Humbeline. She cheered him up and soon Bernard became a very popular man. He was handsome and intelligent, full of fun and good humor. People enjoyed being with him.

Yet one day, Bernard greatly surprised his friends by telling them he was going to join the very strict Cistercian order. They did all they could to make him give up the idea. But in the end, it was Bernard who convinced his brothers, an uncle and twenty-six friends to join him. As Bernard and his brothers left their home, they said to their little brother Nivard, who was playing with other children: "Good-bye, little Nivard. You will now have all the lands and property for yourself." But the boy answered: "What! Will you take heaven and leave me the earth? Do you call that fair?" And not too long after, Nivard, too, joined his brothers in the monastery. St. Bernard became a very good monk. After three years, he was sent to start a new Cistercian monastery and to be its abbot. The new monastery was in the Valley of Light and became known by that name. In French, the Valley of Light is "Clairvaux." Bernard was the abbot there for the rest of his life.

Although he would have liked to stay working and praying in his monastery, he was called out sometimes for special assignments. He preached, made peace between rulers, and went to advise popes. He also wrote beautiful spiritual books. He became the most influential man of his time. Yet Bernard's great desire was to be close to God, to be a.monk. He was not trying to become famous. This saint had a great devotion to the Blessed Mother. It is said that he often greeted her with a "Hail Mary" when he passed her statue. One day, the Blessed Mother returned his greeting: "Hail, Bernard!" In this way, Our Lady showed how much his love and devotion pleased her.

St. Bernard died in 1153. People were saddened because they would miss his wonderful influence. He was proclaimed a saint in 1174 by Pope Alexander III. He was also named a Doctor of the Church in 1830 by Pope Pius VIII.

St. Bernard reminds us that every individual makes a difference. We can all give a wonderful gift of our talents and our energy to make the world better. If you wonder what gifts the Lord is asking of you, you can pray to St. Bernard for help.

AUGUST 21

ST. PIUS X

This great pope's name was Joseph Sarto. He was born in 1835, the son of a mailman in Riese, Italy. Joseph was given the affectionate nickname of "Beppi." When Joseph felt that God wanted him to be a priest, he had to make many sacrifices for his education. But he didn't mind. He even walked miles to school barefoot to save his one good pair of shoes. After he was ordained a priest, Father Sarto labored for the people in poor parishes for seventeen years. Everybody loved him. He used to give away everything he had to help them. His sisters had to hide his shirts or he would have had nothing to wear. Even when Father Joseph became a bishop, and a cardinal, he still gave away what he owned to the poor. He kept nothing for himself.

When Pope Leo XIII died in 1903, Cardinal Sarto was chosen pope. He took the name of Pius X. He became known as the pope who loved the Holy Eucharist. Pope Pius X encouraged everyone to receive Jesus as often as they could. He also made a law permitting young children to receive Holy Communion too. Before that time, boys and girls had to wait many years before they could receive the Lord. He is also the pope of religious instruction. He believed in and loved our Catholic faith. He wanted every Catholic to share in the beauty of the truths of our faith. He really cared about every single person and their spiritual and material needs. He encouraged priests and religion teachers to help everyone learn about their faith.

When the terrible World War I broke out, St. Pius X suffered greatly. He knew so many people would be killed. He had said: "I would gladly give my life to save my poor children from this horrible suffering." Toward the end of his life, he also said: "I have lived poor, and I wish to die poor." He did so much to help the poor that people wondered where all the money came from. He never kept anything for himself, right to the end of his life. Pope Pius X died on August 20, 1914.

The last pope before him to be declared a saint was Pope St. Pius V. Pope Clement X had canonized him in 1672. We celebrate the feast of St. Pius V on April 30. Joseph Sarto, Pope St. Pius X, was proclaimed a saint by Pope Pius XII in 1954.

When we want to deepen our love and reverence for the Holy Eucharist, we can pray to St. Pius X. He was so kind and understanding. He can lead us to love Jesus, Mary and our Catholic faith as he did.

MARY, OUR QUEEN

We can think of today's feast as connected with Mary's Assumption, which we celebrated on August 15. Today we think of Mary with her Son in heaven. She is there with her body as well as her soul.

Even though governments today are often democracies, we can still understand the importance of kings and queens in the history of many countries. A good queen was greatly loved and served with joy. That is the kind of queen Mary, our Mother, is. She is a kind and loving queen. She is our Mother and teacher, too.

As our Mother, Mary takes care of us. We never have to be ashamed to ask her for anything. She will give us spiritual gifts. She will help us with our physical needs. She is also our teacher, because she left us examples of how to be true disciples of Jesus. If we invite Mary to be our queen, she will teach us many wonderful things about the life of Jesus in us. She will take us to her Son.

We can honor Mary every day in several ways. We can whisper a Hail Mary when we are walking along or doing a chore. We can spend some quiet time in our room or another location and say the Rosary. We can keep a little statue or picture of Mary near our bed to remind us to honor her with prayer.

This is the way we make Mary the center and queen of our hearts.

We can say the Hail Mary often throughout the day:

Hail Mary, full of grace, the Lord is with you. Blessed are you among women, and blessed is the fruit of your womb, Jesus. Holy Mary, mother of God, pray for us sinners now and at the hour of our death. Amen.

AUGUST 23

ST. ROSE OF LIMA

This South American saint was born in Lima, Peru, in 1586. Her real name was Isabel, but she was such a beautiful baby that she was called Rose. She received the sacrament of Confirmation from St. Turibius, archbishop of Lima. We celebrate his feast on March 23. As Rose grew older, she became more and more beautiful. One day her mother put a wreath of flowers on her head to show off her loveliness to friends. But Rose was not impressed. She only wanted Jesus to notice her and love her.

Rose did not think she was special because of her own beauty. She realized that beauty is a gift from God. She even became afraid that her beauty might be a temptation to someone. She noticed people staring at her with approval. She heard them say that her complexion was smooth and beautiful. So she did an unusual thing: she rubbed her face with pepper until her skin became all red and blistered. She certainly did not have to worry about receiving compliments for a while.

St. Rose worked hard to support her parents who were very poor. She humbly obeyed them, too, except when they tried to get her to marry. That she would not do. Her love for Jesus was so great that when she talked about him, her face glowed. Rose prayed that her parents would be more accepting of her way of life. She wanted to live for Jesus alone. She had many temptations from the devil. There also were times when she had to suffer terrible loneliness and sadness. During those times, God seemed far away. Yet she cheerfully offered all these troubles to him. She kept praying for her trust to grow stronger. In her last long, painful sickness, this heroic young woman used to pray: "Lord, increase my sufferings, and with them increase your love in my heart." She was just thirty-one when she died on August 24, 1617, in Lima.

St. Rose of Lima was proclaimed a saint by Pope Clement X in 1671. He also named her patroness of the Americas, Philippines and West Indies.

St. Rose of Lima was not fooled by her own physical beauty. She tried to grow spiritually beautiful for Jesus. When we are worried about our looks or our personality, we can ask St. Rose to help us focus on what is really important in our lives.

ST. BARTHOLOMEW

"Bartholomew" was one of the first followers of Jesus. This apostle's other name was Nathaniel. He came from Cana in Galilee. He became a disciple of Jesus when his friend Philip invited him to come and meet the Lord. Nathaniel received high praise from Jesus, who said, as soon as he saw him, "Here is a man in whom there is no guile." Jesus meant that Nathaniel was an honest, sincere man who would never deceive anyone. His one desire was to know the truth.

Nathaniel was very surprised to hear those words from the Lord. "How do you know me?" he asked. "Before Philip called you," Jesus answered, "I saw you under the fig tree." That was a favorite praying-place. Nathaniel must have realized then that Jesus had read his heart as he prayed. "Master!" he cried. "You are the Son of God, the King of Israel." And Nathaniel became one of the Lord's faithful apostles.

Like the other apostles, Nathaniel, or Bartholomew, preached the Gospel of Jesus at the risk of his life. It is believed that he went to India, Armenia and other lands. He preached with great zeal, until he gave his life for the faith. And so, to the reward of an apostle, St. Bartholomew added the martyr's crown.

Jesus admired the honesty of St. Bartholomew. Even though Bartholomew had his opinions, he was not stubborn. So Jesus praised him. He also gave Bartholomew the grace of faith and the vocation to be an apostle.

AUGUST 25

The current Roman calendar lists two saints on August 25. Their stories are briefly presented here one after the other.

ST. LOUIS OF FRANCE

Louis was born on April 25, 1214. His father was King Louis VIII of France and his mother was Queen Blanche. The story is told that when Prince Louis was small, his mother hugged him tightly. She said, "I love you, my dear son, as much as a mother can love her child. But I would rather see you dead at my feet than ever to have you commit a mortal sin." Louis never forgot those words. He grew to cherish his Catholic faith and his upbringing. When he was twelve, his father died and he became the king. Queen Blanche ruled until her son was twenty-one.

Louis became a remarkable king. He married Margaret, the daughter of a count. They loved each other very much. They had eleven children. Louis was a good husband and father. And as long as his mother, Queen Blanche lived, he showed her full respect. Busy as he was, the king found time for daily Mass and the recitation of the Divine Office. He was a Third Order Franciscan and lived a simple lifestyle. He was generous and fair. He ruled his people with wisdom, charity and true Christian principles. There was no separation between what he believed as a Catholic and how he lived. He knew how to settle arguments and disputes. He listened to the poor and the underprivileged. He had time for everybody, not just the rich and influential. He supported Catholic education and built monasteries.

The historian, Joinville, wrote a biography of St. Louis. He recalls that he was twenty-two years in the king's service. He was daily in the king's company. And he could say that he never heard King Louis swear or use any kind of profanity in all those years. Nor did the king permit bad language in his castle.

St. Louis felt an urgent obligation to help the suffering Christians in the Holy Land. He wanted to be part of the Crusades. Twice he led an army against the Turks. The first time, he was taken prisoner. But even in jail, he behaved as a true Christian knight. He was unafraid and noble in all his ways. He was freed and returned to take care of his kingdom in France. Yet as soon as he could, he started back to fight the enemies of the faith again. On the way, however, this greatly loved king contracted typhoid fever. A few hours before he died, he prayed, "Lord, I will enter into your house, worship in your holy temple, and give glory to your name." St. Louis died on August 25, 1270. He was fifty-six years old. He was proclaimed a saint by Pope Boniface VIII in 1297.

It isn't easy to live up to our Christian values at any time in history. St. Louis IX teaches us by his example that we have to make time for God and for prayer. If we are ever tempted to think that we are too busy to pray, we can ask King St. Louis to convince us otherwise.

ST. JOSEPH CALASANZ

Joseph was born in 1556, in his father's castle in Spain. He went to college and became a lawyer. He was ordained a priest at the age of twenty-eight. Joseph was given high positions and he did his work well. Yet he felt that God was calling him to do some special work for poor children in Rome. Obedient to the Lord's call, he gave up everything he had in Spain and went to Rome. There his heart was filled with pity for all the orphans and homeless children he saw everywhere. They were ignorant and neglected. Joseph began to gather them together to teach them all the regular subjects, and especially their religion. Other priests joined him. Soon Joseph became the superior of a new religious order. But he never let his duties as founder and superior stop him from teaching his beloved children. He would even sweep the classrooms himself. He often led the little ones to their homes after school was over.

St. Joseph had much to suffer from people who tried to take over his order. They wanted to run it their way. Once he was even led through the streets like a criminal. He was almost put in jail, although the good priest had done nothing wrong. When he was ninety years old, the saint received terrible news. His order had been forbidden to continue in the way he had started it. Yet despite this suffering, Joseph only said: "The Lord gave and the Lord has taken away. Blessed be the name of the Lord. My work has been done simply out of love for God."

Two years later, in 1648, the saint died a calm, peaceful death. He was ninety-two years old. Several years afterward, his order, the Piarist Fathers, was allowed to continue St. Joseph's wonderful mission. He was proclaimed a saint by Pope Clement XIII in 1767. Pope Pius XII declared him patron of Christian schools in 1948.

Sometimes events or situations turn out differently from what we had planned. We might not be able to understand why. St. Joseph Calasanz shows us how to trust God and be patient. When we find that difficult, we can ask this saint to strengthen us.

ST. ELIZABETH BICHIER

Elizabeth was born in 1773. As a little girl, her favorite game was building castles in the sand. Many years later, this holy French woman had to take charge of building convents for the order of nuns she founded. "I guess building was meant to be my business," she joked, "since I started it so young!" In fact, by 1830, eight years before her death, Elizabeth had already opened over sixty convents.

During the time of the French Revolution, Elizabeth's family lost everything they owned. This was because the republicans were taking property from the nobility. But this intelligent young woman of nineteen studied law so she could fight her family's case in court. When she won and saved her family from ruin, the village shoemaker exclaimed: "All you have to do now is marry a good republican!" Elizabeth, however, had no intention of marrying anyone—republican or noble. On the back of a picture of Our Lady, she had written: "I dedicate and consecrate myself to Jesus and Mary forever."

With the help of St. Andrew Fournet, Elizabeth started a new religious order called the Daughters of the Cross. We celebrate St. Andrew Fournet's feast on May 13. This new order taught children and cared for the sick. Elizabeth would face any danger to help people. Once she found a tramp lying sick in a barn. She brought him to the convent hospital and did all she could for him until he died. The next morning the police chief came to tell her she could be arrested for sheltering a man believed to be a criminal. Elizabeth was unafraid. "I only did what you yourself would have done, sir," she said. "I found this poor sick man, and took care of him until he died. I am ready to tell the judge just what happened." Of course, the saint's honesty and charity won her great respect. People admired her straight, clear answers.

The order's co-founder, St. Andrew Fournet, died in 1834. St. Elizabeth wrote to the sisters, "This is our greatest and most sad loss." St. Elizabeth died on August 26, 1838. She was proclaimed a saint by Pope Pius XII in 1947.

St. Elizabeth Bichier was courageous and energetic. We can pray to her if we realize that we are not as generous in our Christian vocation as we should be. She will help us be generous followers of Jesus.

AUGUST 27

ST. MONICA

It was in Tagaste, northern Africa, that this famous mother of St. Augustine was born in 332. She was brought up as a good Christian. Her strong training was a great help to her when she married the pagan Patricius. Patricius admired his wife, but he made her suffer because of his bad temper. Still Monica never answered back and never complained about him to anyone. Instead she prayed for him fervently. Patricius admitted his belief in Christianity in 371. He was baptized on his deathbed in 372. His mother, too, became a Christian.

St. Monica's joy over the holy way in which her husband had died soon changed to great sorrow. She found out that her son Augustine was living a bad, selfish life. This brilliant young man of nineteen had turned to a false religion and to immoral habits. Monica prayed and cried and did much penance for her son. She begged priests to talk to him. Augustine was brilliant, yet very stubborn. He did not want to give up his sinful life. But Monica would not give up either. When he went to Rome without her, she followed him. At Rome, she found he had become a teacher in Milan. So Monica went to Milan. And in all those years, she never stopped praying for him. What love and faith! After years of prayers and tears, her reward came when Augustine was converted. He not only became a good Christian, as she had prayed. Augustine also became a priest, a bishop, a great writer and a very famous saint.

St. Monica died in Ostia, outside Rome, in 387. Augustine was at her bedside.

We should not become discouraged if our prayers are not answered right away. Like St. Monica, we must keep praying. Jesus tells us in the Gospel to ask and we shall receive.

AUGUST 28

ST. AUGUSTINE

St. Augustine was born in Tagaste in modern Algeria on November 13, 354. This famous son of St. Monica spent many years in wicked living and in false beliefs. He was one of the most intelligent persons who ever lived. Augustine was brought up in a Christian atmosphere by his mother. Unfortunately, he became so proud and immoral that eventually he could not see or understand spiritual truths anymore. His mother Monica prayed daily for her son's conversion. The marvelous sermons of St. Ambrose made their impact too. Finally, Augustine became convinced that Christianity was the true religion. Yet he did not become a Christian then, because he thought he could never live a pure life. One day, however, he heard about two men who had suddenly been converted after reading the life of St. Anthony of the Desert. We celebrate his feast on January 17. Augustine felt ashamed. "What are we doing?" he cried to his friend Alipius. "Unlearned people are taking heaven by force. Yet we, with all our knowledge, are so cowardly that we keep rolling around in the mud of our sins!"

Full of bitter sorrow, Augustine went into the garden and prayed, "How much longer, Lord? Why don't I put an end to my sinning now?" Just then he heard a child singing, "Take up and read!"

Thinking that God intended him to hear those words, he picked up the Bible and opened it. His eyes fell on St. Paul's letter to the Romans, chapter 13. It was just what Augustine needed. Paul says to stop living immoral lives and to live in imitation of Jesus. That did it! From then on, Augustine began a new life.

He was baptized and ordained a priest and bishop. He was a famous Catholic writer and founder of the Augustinian order. He became one of the greatest saints who ever lived. On the wall of his room, he had the following sentence written in large letters: "Here we do not speak evil of anyone." St. Augustine overcame strong heresies, lived simply and supported the poor. He preached very often, and prayed with great fervor right up until his death. "Too late have I loved you," he once cried to God. But Augustine spent the rest of his life in loving God and leading others to love him, too.

Thinking over the lives of the saints, we should tell ourselves, "Can we not do what these men and women did?" We can become saints, too, if we pray for strength to do God's will.

BEHEADING OF
ST. JOHN THE BAPTIST

St. John the Baptist was a cousin of Jesus. His mother was St. Elizabeth and his father was Zechariah. The first chapter of Luke's Gospel tells of the wonderful event of John's birth. Mark's Gospel, chapter 6:14-29, records the cruel details of John the Baptist's death. What harsh consequences John accepted for teaching the truth.

King Herod and his wife refused to hear how they stood with God. They wanted to make their own rules and live their own lives. St. John the Baptist had to pay the price for his honesty. Yet he would have had it no other way. He would never have kept silent while sin and injustice were happening. He called people to repentance and wanted everyone to be reconciled to God. He recognized that true happiness comes from God.

John had preached a baptism of repentance, preparing people for the Messiah. He baptized Jesus in the Jordan River and watched with quiet joy as the Lord's public ministry began. John encouraged his own disciples to follow Jesus. He knew that Jesus' fame would grow, while his would fade away. In the first chapter of the Gospel of John, St. John the Baptist calls himself a voice crying in the desert to make straight the path of the

Lord. He invited people to get ready, to prepare themselves to recognize the Messiah.

His message is the same to each of us.

We can ask St. John the Baptist to help us be always ready to recognize the coming of Jesus into our lives.

ST. PAMMACHIUS

Pammachius was a distinguished Christian layman who lived in the fourth century. As a young student, he had become friends with St. Jerome. They remained friends all their lives and kept an ongoing correspondence. His wife was Paulina, the second daughter of St. Paula, another good friend of St. Jerome. When Paulina died in 397, St. Jerome and St. Paulinus of Nola wrote deeply moving letters filled with sympathy, support and the promise of prayers.

Pammachius was heart-broken about his wife's death. He spent the rest of his life serving in the hospice he and St. Fabiola built. There pilgrims coming to Rome were welcomed and made comfortable. Pammachius and Fabiola willingly accepted and even preferred the poor, the sick and the handicapped. Pammachius felt that his deceased wife was with him as he performed his works of mercy. Paulina had been known for her love for the poor and suffering. Her husband now believed that by caring for them, he was paying the best possible tribute to her memory.

St. Pammachius was much more gentle with his words and ways than the fiery St. Jerome. He often suggested to Jerome that he soften or reword his letters, but Jerome usually did not. For example, a man named Jovinian was teaching serious errors. Jerome wrote a harsh essay exposing Jovinian's errors.

Pammachius read the essay and made some good suggestions about rewording the overpowering expressions. St. Jerome thanked his friend for his concern, but did not make the corrections. Pammachius also tried to heal a quarrel between his friend St. Jerome and a man named Rufinus. But it does not seem that he could move Jerome to become more mild in his handling of the person or issues.

St. Pammachius had a church in his house. Today it is the Passionist church of Saints John and Paul. St. Pammachius died in 410 as the Goths were taking over Rome.

St. Pammachius knew how to be a good friend. He was supportive and honest. We can ask him to help us be true to our friends as he was.

ST. AIDAN

Aidan was a seventh-century Irish monk. He lived at the great monastery of Iona, which St. Columban had founded. St. Oswald became king of North England in 634. He asked for missionaries to preach to his pagan people. The first missionary to go soon came back complaining that the English were rude, stubborn and wild. The monks got together to talk about the situation. "It seems to me," St. Aidan said to the returned monk, "that you have been too harsh with those people." He then explained that, as St. Paul says, first easy teachings are to be given. Then when the people have grown stronger on the Word of God, they can start to do the more perfect things of God's holy law.

When the monks heard such wise words, they turned to Aidan. "You should be the one to go to North England to preach the Gospel," they said. Aidan went willingly. He took on his new assignment with humility and a spirit of prayer. He began by preaching. King St. Oswald himself translated Aidan's sermons into English until the saint learned the language better. St. Aidan traveled all over, always on foot. He preached and helped the people. He did much good and was greatly loved by the people. After thirty years of St. Aidan's ministry, any monk or priest who came into the village was greeted with great joy by all the villagers.

On the island of Lindisfarne, St. Aidan built a large monastery. So many saints were to come from there that Lindisfarne became known as the Holy Island. Little by little, the influence of these zealous missionaries changed North England into a civilized, Christian land.

St. Aidan died in 651.

We can learn from St. Aidan's life that the witness of a joyful, kind person is a powerful influence on others. When we need help seeing the good in people, we can whisper a prayer to St. Aidan.

september

SEPTEMBER 1

ST. GILES

Giles was born in Athens, Greece, in early times. When his parents died, he used the large fortune they left him to help the poor. For this reason and especially because he worked many miracles, Giles found himself a greatly admired young man. He did not want this praise and fame at all. So, to be able to serve God in a hidden life, he left Greece and sailed to France.

There he went to live alone in a dark forest. He made his home in a rough cave behind a thick thorn bush. Giles lived there contented, safe from the danger of becoming conceited at hearing himself praised. But one day, a certain king and his men went hunting the forest. They chased the deer that often came to Giles' cave. The deer lost them by going into Giles' cave, which was hidden behind the large thorn bush. One of the men shot an arrow into the thorn bush, hoping to hit the deer. When they forced their way in, they discovered Giles sitting wounded by the arrow.

"Who are you and what are you doing here?" demanded the king. St. Giles told them the story of his life. When they heard it, they asked his forgiveness. The king sent his doctors to take care of the saint's wound. Although Giles begged to be left alone, the king felt such respect for him that he came often to see him. Giles never would accept the king's gifts. Finally, however, he agreed to let the king build a large monastery there. Giles became its first abbot.

This monastery became so famous that a whole town grew up there. When the saint died, his grave at the monastery became a great shrine where many people came on pilgrimage.

St. Giles realized that only God can make us really happy. The next time we are tempted to be selfish and self-centered, we can pray to St. Giles. He will help us become God-centered and generous with our lives and our time.

SEPTEMBER 2

BLESSED JOHN DU LAU
AND THE SEPTEMBER MARTYRS

Blessed John was the archbishop of Arles, France. He and his companions are celebrated today because they died heroic martyrs' deaths during the French Revolution. The new constitution of 1790 was against the Church. The people were being forced to sign their agreement with an oath. If they did not, they were punished. By 1792, the punishment was more than a prison term. Now it meant death.

Many brave bishops, priests, religious and lay people would not sign the oath supporting the French constitution. They knew they would be betraying God and his Church. Pope Pius VI told them that they were right. It was a sad time for the people of France. On September 2, 1792, a crowd of several hundred people rioted and broke into a former monastery. It was now a prison for priests and religious. The mob approached several priests and told them to sign the oath. Each priest definitely refused. Each was slain on the spot.

Among the martyrs was Blessed Alexander Lenfant, a Jesuit. Just a few minutes before he died, he had been hearing the confession of a fellow priest. Both were killed moments later. The rioters then went to the Carmelite church which was also being used as a prison. Blessed John, archbishop of Arles, and other bishops and priests were being held there. All refused to take the oath and all were murdered. On September 3, the same mob went to the Lazarist seminary. It was also a temporary prison, with ninety priests and religious. Only four escaped death.

By the time the terrible Revolution had ended, 1,500 Catholics had been killed. Several were bishops, priests and religious. The martyrs we celebrate today number 191. They were proclaimed "blessed" in 1926 by Pope Pius XI.

We can ask today's martyrs to help us understand that the precious gift of our Catholic faith has to be cherished. We never want to take our religion for granted.

ST. GREGORY THE GREAT

St. Gregory was born in 540 in Rome. His father was a senator. His mother is a saint, St. Celia. Gregory studied philosophy and while still young, became governor of Rome. When his father died, Gregory turned his large house into a monastery. For several years he lived as a good and holy monk. Then Pope Pelagius made him one of the seven deacons of Rome. When the pope died, Gregory was chosen to take his place. He did not want that honor at all. He was so holy and wise, however, that everyone knew he would be a good pope. Gregory even disguised himself and hid in a cave, but he was found and made pope anyway.

For fourteen years he ruled the Church. Even though he was always sick, Gregory was one of the greatest popes the Church has ever had. He wrote many books and was a wonderful preacher. He cared for people all over the world. In fact, he considered himself the servant of all. He was the first pope to use the title "servant of the servants of God." All the popes since have used this title.

St. Gregory took special, loving care of poor people and strangers. Every day he used to feed them a good dinner. He was also very sensitive to the injustices people suffered. Once, when he was still a monk, he saw some blond boys up for sale in the slave market of Rome. He asked where they were from and was told that they were from England. The saint felt a great desire to go to England to bring the love of Jesus to those pagans. When he became pope, one of the first things he did was to send some of his best monks to convert the English to Christ.

The last years of this holy pope's life were filled with great sufferings, yet he continued working for his beloved Church until the very end. St. Gregory died on March 12, 604.

Every morning we can decide to do at least one good deed of kindness during the day.

SEPTEMBER 4

ST. ROSE OF VITERBO

Rose was born in 1235 in Viterbo, Italy. She lived at the time when Emperor Frederick had conquered land that belonged to the Church. Rose's special mission was to make the people of her own city and nearby cities remain faithful to the Holy Father. And this she did when she was just a teenager.

In fact, Rose was only eight years old when our Blessed Mother told her while she was sick that she was to wear the habit of St. Francis. Our Lady also told Rose to give good example by her words and actions. Slowly the girl gained her health. She began to think more and more about how much

Jesus suffered for us and how much sinners hurt him. She prayed and made sacrifices to show Jesus how much she loved him.

Later on, this daring girl began to preach in the streets of the city. She told people to stand up to the emperor who had taken land from the Church. So many people listened to the saint that Rose's father became frightened. He told her he would beat her if she did not stop preaching. She was only about thirteen, but she answered gently, "If Jesus could be beaten for me, I can be beaten for him. I do what Jesus has told me to do, and I must not disobey him."

Two years more Rose preached with such success that the enemies of the pope wanted her killed. In the end, the ruler sent Rose and her parents out of the city. But she said that the emperor was going to die soon and that is just what happened. Back in Viterbo, the saint was not permitted to become a nun, so she returned to her own home. There she died in 1252, when she was only seventeen. Her body is still preserved and venerated in Viterbo.

In her very short life St. Rose did much good. We can ask her to help us be as energetic and courageous every day as she was.

ST. LAWRENCE JUSTINIAN

Lawrence was born in Venice, Italy, in 1381. His mother sometimes thought her son was aiming too high. He always told her that he wanted to become a saint. When he was nineteen, he felt he should serve God in a special way. He asked the advice of his uncle, a holy priest of the community of St. George. "Do you have the courage to turn down the delights of the world and to live a life of penance?" asked his uncle. Lawrence was quiet a long time. Then he looked up at a crucifix and said, "You, O Lord, are my hope. In this cross there is comfort and strength."

His mother wanted him to marry, but Lawrence joined the community of St. George. His first assignment was to go out among the people of his city and seek donations for the support of the order. Lawrence was not ashamed to beg. He realized that the offerings of money or goods would help God's work. He even went in front of his own home and asked charity. His mother would try to fill up his sack with food, so that he could go back to the monastery early. But Lawrence would only accept two loaves of bread and then would be off to the next house. In this way, he learned how to make little acts of self-denial and grew very dear to God.

One day a friend of his came to try to persuade Lawrence to leave the monastery. Instead, the saint spoke of how short life is and how wise it is to live for heaven. His friend was very impressed and was persuaded to become a religious himself.

Later, Lawrence was made a bishop, even though he was not happy about it. His people soon learned what a kind and holy man their bishop was. Crowds came to him for help every day. When he was dying, he would not lay on a soft bed. "That shall not be!" he exclaimed humbly. "My Lord was stretched out on a hard and painful tree." St. Lawrence Justinian died in 1455.

Let us pray to the Lord today to give holy priests to his Church.

SEPTEMBER 6

BLESSED BERTRAND

Bertrand lived in the last half of the twelfth and first part of the thirteenth centuries. His country, France, was troubled by religious wars. There was great confusion about Church teaching. Bertrand's parents managed to live a peaceful life and they taught the true faith to their son. In 1200, the Cistercian monasteries were attacked by an army led by Raymond of Toulouse. He believed in a heresy called Albigensianism. He attacked people who did not believe as he did. He especially persecuted the Cistercian monks. They were trying very hard to help people know about the true Catholic faith.

Bertrand became a Cistercian and a priest. Around 1208, he met St. Dominic. This was God's invitation to him to begin a very important ministry. He was one of the six men who joined Dominic in 1215 to form a new religious congregation, the Order of Preachers. They are often called "Dominicans" after their founder. Blessed Bertrand was sent to Paris to start the order there. After a short while, St. Dominic called for Friar Bertrand to go to Bologna to establish the order there. Bertrand obeyed happily. Meanwhile, the Order of Preachers was growing. They preached the Gospel message in the towns and countryside. They wanted people to know and love their Catholic faith. In 1219, Blessed Bertrand accompanied St. Dominic on a trip to Paris. He loved and admired St. Dominic very much.

The Dominicans had a big meeting in 1221, called a General Chapter. Bertrand was there. The order was divided into eight provinces so that the religious and their ministries could be more effective. Bertrand was made the superior or provincial of southern France. He spent the rest of his life preaching and helping people grow closer to God. He died in 1230 and was proclaimed "blessed" by Pope Leo XIII in 1881.

When we wonder about what we will do with our lives, we can ask Blessed Bertrand to help us become aware of God's plan for us.

BLESSED JOHN DUCKETT
AND BLESSED RALPH CORBY

This is the second time the name Duckett appears as we go through the calendar of saints and blesseds. James Duckett, an English martyr, is celebrated on April 19. He was related in some way to one of today's martyrs, John Duckett. Both John Duckett and Ralph Corby were priests. They lived in the seventeenth century and died as martyrs for the faith in 1644.

Father John studied at the English college of Douay and became a priest in 1639. He studied for three more years in Paris, and spent several hours each day in prayer. Before being sent back to his persecuted England, he spent two months with the Cistercian monks, devoting that time to prayer and retreat. The young priest labored for a year in England. He was caught with holy oils and a book of rites. When his captors threatened harm to his family and friends if he did not confess his identity, he admitted that he was a priest. He was brought to prison in London. There he met a fellow priest, Ralph Corby, a Jesuit. Father Corby had been laboring in England for twelve years before he was caught celebrating Mass. The Jesuit order tried feverishly to save Father Corby. When the "reprieve" came, he insisted that Father John Duckett who was younger, use it. But Father John would not allow himself to walk away and leave his friend.

Actually, neither priest would have been allowed to take advantage of the reprieve. The judges ignored it and condemned both priests to death. On September 7, 1644, at ten o'clock, the two men mounted the cart that would take them to Tyburn, the scene of execution. Their heads were shaved and they wore their cassocks. Each made a short speech, then embraced each other. They would meet again in the presence of the Lord of glory.

Who can ever really understand why injustices take place? It is hard to forgive when innocent people suffer. When we are angered by injustice, we can pray to Blessed John Duckett and Blessed Ralph Corby. We can ask them to help us be forgiving as they were.

SEPTEMBER 8

BIRTH OF THE
BLESSED VIRGIN MARY

We do not usually celebrate the birthdays of the saints. Instead we celebrate the day they died, because that is the day they were born into the joys of heaven.

But the birthday of Mary, our Blessed Mother, is an exception. We do celebrate her birthday because she came into this world full of grace and because she was to be the Mother of Jesus.

The birth of Our Lady was like a dawn. When the sky starts to turn a rosy pink early in the morning, we know the sun will soon come up. In the same way, when Mary was born, she brought great happiness to the world. Her birth meant that soon Jesus, the Sun of justice, would appear. Mary was the wonderful human being whose privilege it was to bring the Lord Jesus to all people.

Even today, if we have Mary, we have Jesus. Whoever is very devoted to her is very close to the heart of Jesus.

We can make Mary's birthday special by whispering a Hail Mary often throughout the day.

SEPTEMBER 9

ST. PETER CLAVER

This Spanish priest of the Society of Jesus was born in 1580. He is known as the "apostle of the slaves." While he was still studying to become a Jesuit, he felt a burning desire to go to South America as a missionary. He volunteered and was sent to the seaport of Cartagena. There great shiploads of African slaves were brought to be sold.

At the sight of those poor people all crowded together, sick and suffering, Peter felt great pity.

He made up his mind to help them and to convert them. As soon as a shipload arrived, he would go among the hundreds of sick slaves. He gave them food and medicine. He baptized the dying and the little babies. He nursed the ill. It was hard work in terrible heat. One man who went once with St. Peter could never face the heart-breaking sight again. Yet Peter did it for forty years. He baptized some three hundred thousand people. He was there when the ships came in. He cared for and loved those who were treated so unjustly by society.

Although the slave owners tried to stop Father Claver, he taught the faith to the slaves anyway. It was slow, discouraging work. Many people criticized him, saying it was all a waste of time. They thought the slaves would never keep the faith. But St. Peter was patient and he trusted that God would bless his people. He also went to visit his converts after they left Cartagena. The priest never stopped urging the slave owners to take care of the souls of their slaves and to be better Christians themselves.

During the last four years of his life, Father Claver was so sick that he had to stay in his room, He could not even celebrate Mass. Most everyone forgot about him, but he never complained. Then suddenly at his death on September 8, 1654, it was like the whole city woke up. They realized that they had lost a saint. From then on he was never forgotten again. Pope Leo XIII proclaimed him a saint in 1888.

Prejudice against people because of their race, religion, culture or birthplace offends God, the good Father of us all. We can ask St. Peter Claver to help us love everybody as God's children. We can also ask him to help us get rid of any prejudice that could be in our hearts.

SEPTEMBER 10

ST. NICHOLAS OF TOLENTINO

Nicholas was born in 1245 in Ancona, Italy. His parents had waited long and anxiously for a child. Nicholas was the answer to prayer and a pilgrimage the couple had made to the shrine of St. Nicholas of Bari. The couple was so grateful to the saint that they named their baby after him. When the boy grew up, he talked about becoming a priest. He was prayerful and wanted to live close to God. Friends of his family wanted him to be a priest in a wealthy parish where Nicholas would be promoted. Nicholas didn't say much, but he quietly searched and prayed. One day he slipped into a church. A fervent Augustinian priest was preaching a sermon. He said: "Don't love the world or the things of this world because this world is passing away." Nicholas thought about this. He went away with the words dancing in his head. He realized how God had used that preacher to touch his own life. He became convinced of the importance of preaching God's Word. He made up his mind to ask to join the same order to which that priest belonged.

The order was the Augustinian Friars and the priest was Father Reginald who became his novice master. Friar Nicholas professed his vows when he was eighteen. Then he began his studies for the priesthood. He was ordained around 1270. Father Nicholas performed his preaching ministry with love in various parishes. Then while praying in church one day, he seemed to hear a voice saying: "To Tolentino, to Tolentino. Stay there." Shortly afterward, he was assigned to the town of Tolentino. He spent the remaining thirty years of his life there. There was great political unrest in those times. Many people did not come to church to hear the Word and to worship the Lord. The friars of St. Augustine decided that street-preaching was necessary. St. Nicholas was chosen to be part of this initiative. He preached outside and in gathering places willingly. People listened and many repented of their sins and lack of caring. They led better lives. Father Nicholas spent hours in the slum areas of Tolentino. He visited the lonely. He brought the sacraments to the sick and dying. He took care of the needs of children and visited prisoners. Miracles were reported while St. Nicholas was still alive. He touched a diseased child and said, "May the good God make you well," and the child was cured.

St. Nicholas of Tolentino was sick for about a year before he died on September 10, 1305. He was proclaimed a saint by Pope Eugene IV in 1446.

St. Nicholas of Tolentino had been an answer to the prayer of his parents. Because he listened to the call of God in his heart, he could help many people find the Lord. When we would rather "do our own thing," we can ask St. Nicholas of Tolentino to help us be good listeners to the voice of God as he was.

SEPTEMBER 11

BLESSED LOUIS OF THURINGIA

This German prince lived during the last part of the twelfth and first part of the thirteenth centuries. He married St. Elizabeth of Hungary when he was twenty-one and she was just fourteen. The marriage had been arranged by their parents. This was the custom. But they both loved God, and he gave them great love for each other. So it was that they were very happy together. Their joy increased when God sent them their three children. The youngest was Blessed Gertrude.

Louis helped his wife in her many works of charity for the poor. He also joined her in devout prayer. Time after time, the people saw their handsome prince and his lovely wife helping the poor. It is said that once Elizabeth brought a leper into their castle and nursed him in their bed. For a moment, when Louis saw that, he was angry. Then, suddenly, instead of the leper, he saw our crucified Lord lying there. After that proof of how much Jesus appreciated Elizabeth's charity, Louis had a hospital for lepers built.

One long, bitter cold winter, Louis had to be away from his land. When he returned, Elizabeth was overjoyed. The next year Louis left on a Crusade to free the Holy Land from the Muslims. But on the way, he caught malaria, and soon was dying.

Because he had always lived in close union with Jesus, the brave ruler felt no fear of death. He received the Last Sacraments and died peacefully in 1227.

We can ask Blessed Louis to help us recognize occasions today when we can do something good for our family, a friend or a neighbor.

SEPTEMBER 12

ST. EANSWIDA

Eanswida lived in the seventh century. She was the granddaughter of St. Ethelbert, the first Christian king of England. Eanswida's father was Prince Edbald. He was not a religious man at first, but he learned a great deal about Christianity from his little daughter. The girl was devout as well as attractive. Her father had a fine husband selected for her, a pagan prince from Northumbria. Eanswida was not at all pleased. She refused to marry him with good humor so as not to offend her father. He respected her wish and surprised everyone when he permitted his daughter to start a monastery of nuns.

Princess Eanswida was a very happy nun. She lived simply and prayerfully like the rest of the sisters. She spent the rest of her life in penance and prayer for herself and for all the people of her homeland. Eanswida died on the last day of August in 640.

The Danes eventually destroyed her convent, but Benedictine monks started the monastery again in 1095.

Saints remind us that there are lasting values more important than the things of this world. We can ask St. Eanswida to give us some of her wisdom and courage so that we, too, can make wise choices for eternity.

SEPTEMBER 13

ST. JOHN CHRYSOSTOM

St. John Chrysostom was born in Antioch around 344. His father died when he was a baby. His mother chose not to marry again. She gave all her attention to bringing up her son and daughter. She made many sacrifices so that John could have the best teachers. He was very intelligent and could have become a great man in the world. When he gave speeches everyone loved to listen to him. In fact, his name, Chrysostom, means "Golden-mouthed." Yet John wanted to give himself to God. He became a priest and later was made bishop of the great city of Constantinople.

St. John was a wonderful bishop. Although he was always sick, he accomplished a tremendous amount of good. He preached once or twice every day, fed the poor and took care of orphans. He corrected sinful customs and stopped bad plays from being performed. He loved everyone, but he was not afraid to tell even the empress when she did wrong.

Because he fought sin, St. John had enemies—even the empress herself. She had him sent away from Constantinople. On the trip he suffered greatly from fever, from lack of food and sleep. Yet, he was happy to suffer for Jesus. Just before he died, he cried out, "Glory be to God!"

St. John died in Turkey on September 14, 407. A terrible hailstorm fell on Constantinople when he died. Four days later, the evil empress died too. Her son honored St. John's body and showed how sorry he was for what his mother had done.

God sees us all the time. If we do everything as well as we can for him, then we do not have to be afraid of what others say or do against us. We can ask St. John Chrysostom to give us some of his courage.

TRIUMPH OF THE CROSS

Today we celebrate our gratitude and love for Jesus through our respect for the cross. The cross was once the greatest symbol of shame. Criminals who died by the sword were spared the "branding" of crucifixion. Jesus chose to do the most for us to obtain our salvation. He took on the suffering of the cross. With that suffering came the shame.

The cross has become the most sacred Christian symbol. When the cross has the image of the suffering Christ on it, that cross is called a crucifix. The crucifix on our bedroom wall and the crucifix or cross around our neck are important. They remind us that Jesus paid a price for us.

For centuries relics of the true cross have been cherished by devout Christians. It is believed that Emperor Heraclius recovered pieces of wood from the cross of Jesus in 629. He and his group of pilgrims honored the relics and invited all the people in the area to join them. Even before that time, Christians honored and loved the symbol of the cross.

The word "cross" can also mean the sufferings that come our way. When we accept them lovingly and with patience as Jesus did his cross, we become "cross-bearers" like Jesus.

We consider what the symbol of the cross means to us Christians. We might like to say the following short prayer today:

We adore you, O Christ, and we praise you, because by your holy cross you have redeemed the world.

SEPTEMBER 15

OUR LADY OF SORROWS

Our Lady had many great joys as the mother of Jesus, but she had much to suffer, too. Her great love for her divine Son caused Mary to suffer when she saw Jesus treated cruelly by his enemies. Mary is the queen of martyrs because she went through spiritual torments greater than the bodily agonies of the martyrs. Her heart was like an altar when on Calvary she offered up her beloved Jesus to save us. What a terrible suffering it was for so loving a mother to see her Son die on the cross.

There are seven times of great suffering in Mary's life. The first was when she took Baby Jesus to the temple. There the prophet Simeon told her that a sword of suffering would pierce her heart. This would be when Jesus would be put to death. Her second sorrow was when she and St. Joseph had to flee to Egypt with Jesus. Herod's soldiers were trying to kill him. The third suffering came when Mary searched three days in Jerusalem for Jesus. She finally found him in the temple. Our

Lady's fourth sorrow was when Jesus was whipped and crowned with thorns. Her fifth great pain was caused by his being lifted on the cross, where he died after three hours of agony. Mary's sixth sorrow was the moment when Our Lord's sacred body was placed in her arms. And her seventh suffering came when he was buried in the tomb.

Mary did not pity herself or complain because she had to suffer so much during her life. Instead, she offered her sorrows to God for our sakes. She is our Mother. Because she loves us dearly, she was happy to suffer that we might some day share her joy with Jesus in heaven.

In honor of Our Lady of Sorrows, today we can offer up some little sacrifice without complaining. We can also think about each of the seven sorrows of Mary and thank her for her great love for us.

SEPTEMBER 16

ST. CORNELIUS AND ST. CYPRIAN

In the middle of the third century, the Church was still being persecuted. The fierce persecution of Emperor Decius claimed the life of Pope St. Fabian. The Church was without a pope for nearly a year. A holy priest of Rome, Cornelius, was elected in 251. He accepted because he loved Christ. He would serve the Church as pope even if his ministry would cost him his life. That is why Pope Cornelius was so greatly admired throughout the world. The bishops of Africa were especially outspoken in their love and loyalty to the pope. Bishop Cyprian of Carthage sent him letters of encouragement and support. Cyprian had been a convert at the age of twenty-five. He had astonished the Christians of Carthage by pledging a vow of perpetual chastity right before his baptism. He had eventually become a priest and in 249 a bishop.

Bishop Cyprian greatly encouraged Pope Cornelius by reminding him that during the present persecution in Rome not a single Christian had given up the faith. St. Cyprian's writings explain the love that Christians should have for the whole Church. This love should be for the pope as well as for the local diocese and parish. Cyprian wrote a scholarly work on the unity of the Church. This remains an important topic for all times, including our own.

Pope St. Cornelius died in exile at the port of Rome in September, 253. Because he suffered so much as pope, he is considered a martyr. St. Cyprian died five years later during the persecution of Valerian. He was beheaded at Carthage on September 14, 258. Together they share a feast day to remind us of the unity that the Church should always enjoy. This unity is a mark of the presence of Jesus who is the Center.

We can ask Pope St. Cornelius and Bishop St. Cyprian to help us grow in our love for the Church—for the pope, bishops, priests, lay people everywhere.

ST. ROBERT BELLARMINE

Robert was born in Italy in 1542. As a boy, he was not interested in playing games. He liked to spend his time repeating to his younger brothers and sisters the sermons he had heard. He also liked to explain the lessons of the catechism to the little farm children of the neighborhood. Once he had made his first Holy Communion, he used to receive Jesus every Sunday.

Robert's father hoped to make a famous gentleman out of his son. For this reason, he wanted him to study many subjects and music and art, too. Whenever a song had words that were not nice, Robert would make up decent words of his own.

It was his great desire to become a Jesuit priest, but his father had different plans for him. For a whole year, Robert worked to persuade his father. At last, when he was eighteen, he was permitted to join the Jesuits. As a young Jesuit, he did very well in his studies. He was sent to preach even before he became a priest. When one good woman first saw such a young man, not even a priest yet, going up into the pulpit to preach, she knelt down to pray. She asked the Lord to help him not become frightened and stop in the middle. When he finished his sermon, she stayed kneeling. This time, however, she was thanking God for the magnificent sermon.

St. Robert Bellarmine became a famous writer, preacher and teacher. He wrote thirty-one important books. He spent three hours every day in prayer. He had a deep knowledge of sacred matters. Yet even when he had become a cardinal, he considered the catechism so important, that he himself taught it to his household and to the people.

Cardinal Bellarmine died on September 17, 1621. He was proclaimed a saint in 1930 by Pope Pius XI. In 1931, the same pope declared St. Robert Bellarmine a Doctor of the Church.

We can ask St. Robert to help us realize how important our religious instruction classes are. He will help us to be on time for classes, do our homework and put our whole selves into the study of our faith.

SEPTEMBER 18

ST. JOSEPH OF CUPERTINO

Joseph was born on June 17, 1603, in a small Italian village to poor parents. He was very unhappy as a boy and a teenager. His mother considered him a nuisance and treated him harshly. Joseph soon became very slow and absentminded. He would wander around as if he were going nowhere. But he had a temper, too, and so he was not very popular. He tried to learn the trade of shoe-making, but failed. He asked to become a Franciscan, but they would not accept him. Next, he joined the Capuchin order, but eight months later he was advised to leave. He could not seem to do anything right. He dropped piles of dishes and kept forgetting to do what he was told. His mother was not at all pleased to have the eighteen-year-old Joseph back home again. She finally got him accepted as a helper at the Franciscan monastery. He was given the Franciscan habit to wear and was assigned to care for the horses.

About this time, Joseph began to change. He grew more humble and gentle. He became more careful and successful at his work. He also began to do more penance. It was decided that he could become a member of the order and could start studying to become a priest. Although he was very good, he still had a hard time with studies. But Joseph trusted in God's help and he was ordained a priest. God began to work miracles through Father Joseph. Over seventy times people saw him rise from the ground while saying Mass or praying. He would be suspended near the ceiling like a star at the top of a Christmas tree. Often he went into ecstasy and would be completely wrapped up in talking with God. He became very holy. Everything he saw made him think of God.

Father Joseph became so famous for his miracles that he was kept hidden. This made him happy for the chance to be alone with his beloved Lord. Jesus never left him alone and one day came to bring him to heaven. Joseph died in 1663 at the age of sixty. He was proclaimed a saint in 1767 by Pope Clement XIII.

Maybe we feel that our parents, our teachers and even we ourselves think we are not very special. We might put ourselves down. That is when we can pray to St. Joseph Cupertino. He will help us have confidence in ourselves. He will remind us that Jesus lives in our hearts and that we are very special to him.

ST. JANUARIUS

Januarius lived in the fourth century. He was born either in Benevento or Naples, Italy. He was the bishop of Benevento when Diocletian's persecution began. The people of Naples have claimed a special love for and devotion to Bishop Januarius. He is popularly called "San Gennaro." According to common belief, San Gennaro learned that some Christian deacons had been put in prison for their faith. The bishop was a gentle, compassionate man. He truly cared about his people and went to the prison to visit them. The jailer reported him to the governor who sent soldiers to find San Gennaro. The bishop was arrested along with a deacon and a lector. They joined the other prisoners.

San Gennaro and the six others were martyred for their faith. Their deaths took place near Naples in 305. The people of Naples have claimed a special love for and devotion to "San Gennaro." In fact, he is considered their patron saint.

The people of Naples remember San Gennaro for another special reason: his martyr's blood was preserved centuries ago in a vile. The blood has become dark and dry. But at certain times of the year, the blood liquifies. It becomes red, sometimes bright red. At times, it even bubbles. The special case containing the vile of blood is honored publicly on the first Saturday of May, on September 19 (the feast of San Gennaro), within the octave (or eight days after the feast), and at times on December 16. The liquified blood has been seen and honored since the thirteenth century.

We can ask San Gennaro to give us loving, compassionate hearts so that we can bring joy and comfort to the people around us as he did.

SEPTEMBER 20

ST. ANDREW KIM TAEGON AND ST. PAUL CHONG HASANG

St. Andrew Kim Taegon was a priest and St. Paul Chong Hasang was a lay person. These two martyrs represent 113 Catholics who died for their faith in Korea. They were proclaimed saints by Pope John Paul II during his visit to Korea in 1984.

Christianity reached Korea in the seventeenth century. It was brought there by lay people. The believers nourished their faith on the Word of

God. They quietly grew and flourished. Missionary priests came from France. The Korean people were introduced to the sacramental life of the Church. Government persecutions took place, off and on, throughout the nineteenth century. A total of 103 Koreans were killed between 1839 and 1867. Ten members of the Foreign Mission Society of Paris were martyred, too, three bishops and seven priests. This brought the total to 113.

St. Andrew Kim Taegon and St. Paul Chong Hasang represent the glorious and courageous Korean Catholics who paid the price for their love for Christ. St. Andrew Kim Taegon was the first Korean priest. He was martyred on September 16, 1846, just a year after his ordination. Andrew's father had been martyred in 1821. St. Paul Chong Hasang was a heroic lay catechist. He was martyred on September 22, 1846.

Today the Church is growing rapidly in Korea. The gift of faith is being received because of the sacrifice of the martyrs who paved the way.

Every martyr preaches a lesson without ever saying a single word. We look at the death of a martyr and we hear the message. We want to ask the Korean martyrs to help us love Jesus and his Church as much as they did.

ST. MATTHEW

Matthew was a tax collector in the city of Capernaum, where Jesus was living. He was a Jew but he was working for the Romans, who had conquered the Jews. For this reason, his countrymen disliked him. They would not have anything to do with these "public sinners," as tax collectors like Matthew were called.

But Jesus did not feel that way about Matthew. One day, Jesus saw Matthew sitting in his office and he said, "Follow me." At once, Matthew left his money and his position to follow Jesus. He seemed so holy and king-like. Matthew gave a big supper for Jesus. He invited other friends like himself to meet Jesus and listen to him teach. Some people found fault with Jesus for sharing a meal with those whom they considered sinners. However, Jesus had a ready answer. "They who are well do not need a doctor; the sick do. I have not come to call the just, but sinners to repentance."

When Jesus went back to heaven, St. Matthew stayed in Palestine. He remained there for some time to preach about the Lord. We are familiar with the Gospel of Matthew, which is the story of Jesus and what he taught. St. Matthew presents Jesus to his own people. The Lord is the Messiah whom the prophets had said would come to save us.

After preaching the Gospel to many people, St. Matthew ended his life as a glorious martyr for the faith.

When we start to label people as "bad" or as "sinners," it's time for us to say a prayer to St. Matthew. We can ask him to help us avoid labels. We don't want to imitate the wrong things people might do, but we don't want to look down on them either. We just say no to sin and we leave the judgment of people up to God.

ST. THOMAS OF VILLANOVA

Thomas was born in Spain in 1488. From his kind parents, he learned to be very charitable with the poor. He did well in school and became a teacher of philosophy when he finished his studies. Next he joined the Augustinian order. After he became a priest, he was given many important responsibilities. Finally, he was made archbishop of the city of Valencia.

His priests tried to convince him to change his old, mended habit for more dignified robes. However, St. Thomas told them his old clothes had nothing to do with his duty. He would take good care of the spiritual needs of his people. Every day he fed hundreds of poor people. When he received a large sum of money to buy furniture for his house, he gave it to a hospital, saying, "What does a poor monk like me want with furniture?" No wonder he was called the "father of the poor"!

St. Thomas was very gentle with sinners at a time when most people were not. Once when he tried to encourage one man to change his sinful ways, the man angrily insulted him and stormed out of the room. "It was my fault," said the humble archbishop. "I told him a little too roughly." Never would he permit anyone to criticize someone who wasn't there. "He may have had a good reason for doing what he did," the saint would say. "I, for one, believe he did."

Before he died, St. Thomas of Villanova gave to the poor everything he had. He even directed that his bed be sent to the jail for prisoners to use.

St. Thomas died in 1555. He was proclaimed a saint by Pope Alexander VII in 1658.

We can remember St. Thomas of Villanova's words when we need to be more generous. He used to say: "If you want God to hear your prayers, you should help those who are in need."

SEPTEMBER 23

ST. THECLA

Thecla was a beautiful young pagan noble-woman who lived in the first century. She was from the city of Iconium, in Turkey. She read many philosophy books, yet nothing satisfied her desire to know about her Creator. When St. Paul the apostle came to preach the Gospel of Jesus in Iconium, Thecla's prayer to know the one, true God was answered. From St. Paul she also learned that a young woman can become the bride of Christ if she gives up marriage. By this time, Thecla desired nothing else than to give herself entirely to God.

Thecla's pagan parents tried their best to make her give up her Christian faith, but she would not. Her fiancé, Thamyris, begged her not to break their engagement. However, Thecla had made up her mind. She wanted to be Christ's bride, not his. At last, in great anger, Thamyris accused her to the judge. When she still refused to give up her love for Jesus, she was ordered to be burned to death. The beautiful young woman bravely prepared to die. However, it is said that no sooner had the fire been lit than a storm from heaven put it out. Later, she was condemned to be eaten by lions. Once again, however, God saved Thecla's life. Instead of clawing her, the fierce beasts walked gently up to her, lay down at her side, and licked her feet, like pet kittens. At last, in fear, the judge set Thecla free. She went to live in a cave where she spent the rest of her long life. She prayed and taught the people who came to visit her about the Lord Jesus.

If we want to deepen our faith in and love for Jesus, we can ask him for the help we need to live each day generously. When we feel like taking it easy, we can ask St. Thecla to give us some of her courage and energy.

SEPTEMBER 24

ST. PACIFICUS

A little Italian boy born in 1653 was named Charles Anthony. He was just five years old when his loving parents died. He was sent to live with his uncle. This uncle was a cross, mean man. He treated Charles worse than a servant. Yet the boy took this hard treatment quietly and patiently. When he was seventeen, Charles entered a monastery. He chose the name Pacificus, which means "peaceful." After he became a priest, he was made a teacher, but his great desire was to become a preacher. How happy he was when his superior sent him on a preaching mission to many little towns and villages.

St. Pacificus was very popular with people in the country because his talks were simple and gentle. Besides that, he had the marvelous gift of reading consciences. Once, he reminded a man in confession that he had been unkind to his mother. He had also kept impure thoughts in his mind. What Father Pacificus said was true. The man was very sorry for his sins. Everywhere the priest went to preach and hear confessions, he did much good.

But when he had been preaching only about six years, Pacificus had to give it up because of ill health. He became blind, deaf and crippled. He spent his time praying and doing penance in his monastery. He helped others in any way he could. God was always very close to him. He gave him the gift of prophecy. St. Pacificus foretold the great victory of the Christian armies over the Turks at Belgrade. He also said to a bishop, "Your Excellency—heaven! Heaven! And I will follow you soon!" About two weeks later, the bishop died. Not long after, just as he had said, St. Pacificus died, too. It was the year 1721. Many miracles took place at his grave. Father Pacificus was proclaimed a saint by Pope Gregory XVI in 1839.

St. Pacificus had a sad childhood. He could have let himself become an angry, frustrated adult. Instead, he prayed to Jesus for a forgiving, patient heart. His hard times were turned into moments of growing in his love for God and people. Because he had suffered, he could sympathize with the hurts of others and help them to find God in their lives. When we are upset or hurt, we can ask St. Pacificus to help us be like him.

ST. SERGIUS

This famous Russian saint lived in the four-teenth century. He was given the name of Bartholomew when he was baptized. He was not as bright as his two brothers, but he did learn to read and write. This made him very happy be-cause he greatly desired to read the Bible. Bartholomew's parents were nobles. While he was still a boy, the family had to flee from enemies. They had to go to work as peasants. After his parents died, Sergius and his brother Stephen went off to live as hermits. They built a little church from trees they had cut down. The church was dedicated to the Most Holy Trinity.

When his brother went to Moscow to enter a monastery, Bartholomew lived alone. He wore the habit of a monk and took the name Sergius. He was a tall, husky young man. He was strong enough to stand the biting cold and fierce winds of his forest home. He was happy praying to God and loving him with all his heart. He called fire and light his companions, and even made friends with bears.

Before too long, other young men came to share St. Sergius's holy life. They asked him to be their abbot and he did. He was ordained a priest and ruled his monastery very wisely. Once when some of the monks together with his own brother Stephen—who had come back—disagreed with

Sergius, he went away so as to keep peace. Four years later, he was asked to return. The monks were so happy to see him that they kissed his hands, his feet and even his robe. Powerful rulers often went to ask St. Sergius for advice. He became so famous that he was asked to become bishop of the greatest Russian diocese. But he was too humble to accept. The prince of Moscow was not sure if he should try to fight the terrible pagan Tartars. St. Sergius said, "Do not fear, sir. Go forward with faith against the foe. God will be with you." And the Russians were victorious.

It was not great learning that made people trust and love St. Sergius. It was his confidence in God and his desire to help everybody. St. Sergius died in 1392.

When someone disagrees with us or starts an argument, we can remember that the same thing happened to St. Sergius. We can ask him to help us keep calm and remain peaceful.

SEPTEMBER 26

ST. COSMAS AND ST. DAMIEN

These two martyrs were twin brothers from Syria who lived in the fourth century. They were very famous students of science and both became excellent doctors. Cosmas and Damien saw in every patient a brother or sister in Christ. For this reason, they showed great charity to all and treated their patients to the best of their ability. Yet no matter how much care a patient required, neither Cosmas nor Damien ever accepted any money for their services. For this reason, they were called by a name in Greek which means "the penniless ones."

Every chance they had, the two saints told their patients about Jesus Christ, the Son of God. Because the people all loved these twin doctors, they listened to them willingly. Cosmas and Damien often brought health back to both the bodies and the souls of those who came to them for help.

When Diocletian's persecution of Christians began in their city, the saints were arrested at once. They had never tried to hide their great love for their Christian faith. They were tortured, but nothing could make them give up their belief in Christ. They had lived for him and had brought so many people to his love. So at last, they were put to death in the year 303. These holy martyrs are named in the First Eucharistic Prayer of the Mass.

In honor of St. Cosmas and St. Damien, we can perform a work of mercy today—either spiritual or material.

ST. VINCENT DE PAUL

Vincent, the son of poor French peasants, was born in 1581. When he grew up and became famous, he loved to tell people how he had taken care of his father's pigs. Because he was intelligent, his father sent him to school. And after finishing his studies, Vincent became a priest.

At first, he was given an important position as the teacher of rich children, and he lived rather comfortably. Then one day, he was called to the side of a dying peasant. In front of many people, this man declared that all his past confessions had been bad ones. Suddenly Father Vincent realized how badly the poor people of France needed spiritual help. When he began to preach to them, crowds went to confession. He finally decided to start a congregation of priests to work especially among the poor.

The charities of St. Vincent de Paul were so many that it seems impossible for one person to have begun so much. He took care of criminals who worked on the sailing ships. He started the Congregation of the Sisters of Charity with St. Louise de Marillac. He opened hospitals and homes for orphans and old people. He collected large sums of money for poor areas, sent missionaries to many countries, and bought back prisoners from the Mohammedans. Even though he was such a charitable man, however, he humbly admitted that he was not so by nature. "I would have been hard, rough and ill-tempered," he said "were it not for God's grace." Vincent de Paul died in Paris on September 27, 1660. He was proclaimed a saint in 1737 by Pope Clement XII.

Jesus asks us to be good to others, especially to those who suffer. He says to us too, "As long as you did it to one of the least of my brethren, you did it to me."

ST. LAWRENCE RUIZ
AND COMPANIONS

Today's celebration honors a lay person from the Philippines, St. Lawrence Ruiz, and his fifteen companions. These sixteen martyrs were killed for their faith in 1637, in Nagasaki, Japan. Born in Manila, St. Lorenzo was the father of a family. He joined the Dominican priests, brothers and lay volunteers who were going to Japan to preach the Gospel. The group was made up of nine Dominican priests, two brothers, two single lay women, and three other lay persons. All were associated with the Dominican order and all died rather than give up their faith in Jesus. They were missionaries who had originally come from five nations— France, Italy, Japan, the Philippines and Spain.

What a wonderful reminder they are that the Church reaches out to the whole world.

These martyrs suffered greatly before they died, but they would not give up their Catholic religion. It is recorded that St. Lawrence Ruiz told his judges that if he had a thousand lives to give for Christ, he would.

This group of heroes was proclaimed saints by Pope John Paul II on October 18, 1987.

Let us ask St. Lawrence Ruiz and his companion martyrs to inspire the people who are living now to be fervent and generous followers of Jesus.

SEPTEMBER 29

ST. MICHAEL, ST. GABRIEL, ST. RAPHAEL

Michael, Gabriel and Raphael are called "saints" because they are holy. But they are different from the rest of the saints because they were not human. They are angels. They are protectors of human beings and we know something about each of them from the Bible.

Michael's name means "who is like God?" Three books of the Bible speak of St. Michael: Daniel, Revelation and the Letter of Jude. In the book of Revelation or the Apocalypse, chapter 12:7-9, we read of a great war that went on in heaven. Michael and his angels battled with Satan.

Michael became the champion of loyalty to God. We can ask St. Michael to make us strong in our love for Jesus and in our practice of the Catholic religion.

Gabriel's name means "the power of God." He, too, is mentioned in the book of Daniel. He has become familiar to us because Gabriel is an important person in Luke's Gospel. This archangel announced to Mary that she was to be the mother of our Savior. Gabriel announced to Zechariah that he and St. Elizabeth would have a son and call him John. Gabriel is the announcer, the communicator of the Good News. We can ask him to help us be good communicators as he was.

Raphael's name means "God has healed." We read the touching story of Raphael's role in the Bible's book of Tobit. He brought protection and healing to the blind Tobit. At the very end of the journey, when all was completed, Raphael revealed his true identity. He called himself one of the seven who stands before God's throne. We can ask St. Raphael to protect us in our travels, even for short journeys, like going to school. We can also ask him to help when illness strikes us or someone we love.

We can say a short prayer to these three archangels often throughout the day:

St. Michael, St. Gabriel, St. Raphael, be with me today. Protect me from whatever could cause spiritual or physical harm. Help me be faithful to Jesus and a good communicator of his divine love. Amen. (Or, you may prefer to make up your own prayer).

ST. JEROME

Jerome was a Roman Christian who lived in the fourth century. His father taught him his religion well, but sent him to a famous pagan school. There Jerome grew to love pagan writings and lost some of his love for God. Yet, in the company of a group of holy Christians, with whom he became great friends, his heart was turned completely to God.

Later, this brilliant young man decided to live alone in a wild desert. He was afraid that his love for pagan writings would lead him away from the love of God. He welcomed the hard penance and the scorching hot desert. Yet even there, he suffered terrible temptations. The immoral entertainment held in Rome seemed fresh in his imagination and memory. Jerome did not give in, however. He increased his acts of penance and wept for his sins. He also went to study Hebrew with a monk as his teacher. This he did to get rid of the bad thoughts that kept attacking his mind. He became such a great scholar of Hebrew that he could later translate the Bible into Latin. Many more people were then able to read and enjoy it.

St. Jerome spent long years of his life in a little cave at Bethlehem, where Jesus had been born. There he prayed, studied the Bible, and taught many people how to serve God. He wrote a great many letters and even books to defend the faith from heretics.

St. Jerome had a bad temper, and his sharp tongue made him many enemies. Yet he was a very holy man who spent his life trying to serve Jesus in the best way he could. And so, despite his temper, he became a great saint. He died in 419 or 420.

To overcome his strong temptations, St. Jerome worked and studied hard. He also read the Bible. We can imitate Jerome's wonderful habits of hard work, serious study, and frequent reading of the Bible.

Saint Theresa of the Child Jesus

OCTOBER

ST. THERESA OF THE CHILD JESUS

St. Theresa, often called the Little Flower, was born in Normandy, France, in 1873. She was the youngest of the five daughters born to Louis and Zelie Martin. Theresa was a very lively, lovable little girl. Her father called her his "little queen." Yet she could be too sensitive and irritable. In the story she wrote of her life, she tells how the Infant Jesus helped her overcome this weakness.

It was Theresa's great desire to enter the Carmelite convent where two of her sisters were already nuns. But since she was only fifteen, permission was not granted. Theresa felt sure that Jesus wanted her to spend her life loving him alone. She kept praying and asking the superior to admit her. She even dared to ask Pope Leo XIII himself to grant her heart's desire. And finally she was allowed to enter.

Although she was only fifteen, Theresa did not expect to be babied. "Obedience, prayer and sacrifice" were her program. She had a thirst to suffer for love of God. Theresa had the spiritual courage of a real heroine. "May Jesus make me a martyr of the heart or of the body—or better, both!" she wrote. And she meant it. In winter she suffered from the bitter cold and dampness of her plain bedroom. There were other kinds of sufferings, too. Whenever she was humiliated, she would offer her pain to her beloved Jesus. She would hide her hurts under a smile. She told Jesus to do with her whatever was his will.

Sister Theresa tried hard to be humble. She called her great confidence in God her "little way" to holiness. She always had a burning desire to become a saint. The young nun wanted to find a "short cut," an "elevator," to take her quickly to sanctity. So she looked in the Bible, and found the words, "Whoever is a little one, come to me." When she lay dying, she could say: "I have never given the good God anything but love, and it is with love that he will repay. After my death, I will let fall a shower of roses. I will spend my heaven doing good on earth." The Little Flower died on September 30, 1897. She was proclaimed a saint by Pope Pius XI in 1925.

St. Theresa taught us her "little way." Yes, it is a small and yet a great thing to offer our small sacrifices joyfully to Jesus throughout each day.

OCTOBER 2

GUARDIAN ANGELS

Today we celebrate God's messengers who protect us human beings. We see them throughout the Bible. Angels delivered messages from God, protected people from dangers and rescued them. The New Testament Acts of the Apostles tells in chapter 12 how St. Peter was led out of prison by an angel. The belief that we each have a guardian angel has been common to Christians for many centuries.

The picture of a guardian angel that we often see is an angel protecting a little child as he or she walks over a small bridge. In 1608, Pope Paul V added today's feast to the calendar of saints and celebrations. It is very encouraging to know and believe that we each have an angel guarding and protecting us. Our guardian angel is a gift from our loving God.

We can say this brief prayer as often as we would like to throughout the day:

Angel of God, my guardian dear, to whom God's love entrusts me here. Ever this day be at my side, to light and guard, to rule and guide. Amen.

OCTOBER 3

ST. GERARD OF BROGNE

Gerard was born at the end of the ninth century in France. His family was wealthy, but Gerard was not proud. In fact, he was known because of his friendly, kind ways. After a hunting trip, he and his friends returned to his estate tired and hungry. After he invited the others inside for refreshments and rest, he left. Gerard went out and slipped into a little chapel that was on his property. He prayed for a long time. His tired body seemed rested and he forgot all about his hunger.

The idea occurred to Gerard that if people only realized the joy of praying, they would be so much more willing to pray. Then he thought about the monks who spend their life praising God. Imagine how privileged they are, he thought. He prayed over the possibility of a religious vocation and joined the monastery of Saint-Denis.

Gerard loved the life he had chosen and after studies became a priest. He had been a monk for eleven years when he was given permission to start a monastery on his own property at Brogne. The monastery flourished but Gerard felt there was too much activity and excitement. He built himself a little hermitage next to the church. He lived there quietly and alone. But he was not allowed to stay in peace for very long. His superiors asked Gerard to visit the monasteries in Flanders and Normandy.

The monks needed some guidance and help in becoming more fervent. This work took Gerard on many journeys for some twenty years.

All of his life Gerard lived a strict life filled with sacrifices. He did this because he wanted to show Jesus that he loved him. He showed that love by willingly offering little acts of self-denial. When he knew his life on earth was nearly over, he asked to be able to return to his little hut back in Brogne. He was given permission to do that. Gerard died peacefully on October 3, 959.

Gerard shows us by his life that happiness comes from God. We can ask St. Gerard of Brogne to help us look into our hearts to see if we are full of the love of Jesus.

OCTOBER 4

ST. FRANCIS OF ASSISI

Francis was born around 1181. As a young man in his Italian hometown of Assisi, he loved parties and good times. He was handsome and rich, so he bought himself the finest clothes and spent money freely. Francis had no desire to study or to learn his father's business—he just wanted to have fun. After two illnesses and other adventures, Francis realized that he was wasting precious time. He became aware that he should be serving Jesus. He began by praying more and making sacrifices to grow strong in spirit. Once he kissed a horrible-looking leper, while giving him money. Often he gave his clothes and money to the poor. He served the sick in hospitals. Still he felt he must do more. He fasted and began to go around in rags to humble himself.

It is not hard to imagine how his former rich friends must have looked at him now! His father was so angry that he beat him and locked him up at home. Francis bore all this suffering for love of Jesus. When his father took everything from him in disgust, Francis put all his trust in his Father in heaven. He said that he was married to "Lady Poverty" and he began to live as a beggar. He had no shelter. His food was what kind people gave him. Everywhere he went, he urged people to stop sinning and return to God. Soon many men began to realize how close to God this poor man was, and they became his disciples. That is how the great Franciscan order of priests and brothers began. They helped the poor and sick and preached everywhere. Even after the order had spread all over Italy, Francis insisted that they should not own anything. He wanted the friars to love poverty as he did.

St. Francis had the power of working miracles and even of making birds and animals obey him! As a reward for his great love, Jesus gave him his own wounds in his hands and feet. The humble Francis tried to hide them.

Toward the end of his life, he became very sick. He was told he would live only a few more weeks. Then he exclaimed, "Welcome, Sister Death!" He asked to be laid on the ground and covered with an old habit. Then he urged his brothers to love God, to love being poor, and to obey the Gospel. "I have done my part," he said. "May Jesus teach you to do yours." Francis died on October 3, 1226. He was proclaimed a saint a short time later by Pope Honorius III.

St. Francis wanted to be happy more than anything in life. He found happiness when he made Jesus the center of his life. We can ask St. Francis to show us what is really valuable in our lives and what is not.

OCTOBER 5

ST. FLORA OF BEAULIEU

This French saint lived in the fourteenth century. She came from a loving family and joined a convent of nuns at Beaulieu in 1324. She was an innocent, good girl who had resisted her parents' plans for her to marry. But once she gave herself to God as his spouse, he allowed her to prove her love by overcoming all kinds of trials and temptations.

Sometimes it seemed to Sister Flora that she was leading too comfortable a life. At other times, it was too hard. She would be tempted to return home to enjoy herself.

Yet, because she kept trying to love God, Sister Flora grew dearer and dearer to him. At last, he blessed her with wonderful visions and the gift of knowing the future. Soon, people realized that Sister Flora was very holy. They came to ask for prayers and advice.

This saint also received the privilege of suffering the pain of Christ's cross. She seemed to feel it pressing into her, making a wound in her side. She joyfully accepted this suffering out of her great love for Jesus.

Our goals and high ideals will never be reached without sacrifice and dedication. Sometimes we may slip and look for shortcuts. It is then that we can ask St. Flora to give us some of her generosity and courage.

OCTOBER 6

The current Roman calendar lists a saint and a blessed on October 6. Their stories are briefly presented here one after the other.

ST. BRUNO

Bruno was born around 1030. This founder of the Carthusian order of monks was at first not a hermit at all. For eighteen years he was a professor of theology in his own country of France. He tried his best to bring his students closer to God. Then he was given an important position in the diocese of Rheims.

But Bruno was not impressed with the honors or frightened by responsibilities. He became aware that his heart was longing to be alone with Jesus. St. Hugh of Grenoble gave Bruno and his friends a hidden desert land called Chartreuse. There they built a church and little huts to live in. This was the beginning of the Carthusian order. They were very happy there, working their fields, fasting and praying, hidden in God.

After six years, however, Pope Urban II, one of Bruno's former students, required a great sacrifice of him. He asked him to go to Rome to be his advisor. It broke the saint's heart, but he obeyed. He left one of the monks in charge at Chartreuse. Bruno served Pope Urban II well. Then finally he was allowed to live his monk's life nearer to Rome. So with new disciples, Bruno began all over again in Calabria, Italy.

As we know by his letters, St. Bruno was always a cheerful, active man. He did not want to see any of his monks sad. He describes their hard life in delightful expressions. Bruno urged a close friend to come see for himself.

St. Bruno died in 1101. His order continues today. It is the only religious order in the Church that has never had to be reformed. The followers of St. Bruno keep his loving, self-sacrificing spirit alive.

God loves those who serve him with joy. St. Bruno used to say, "Try and you will see how rewarding it is to serve God with all the love of your heart." When we find something to complain about, we can ask St. Bruno to help us change our attitude into joy.

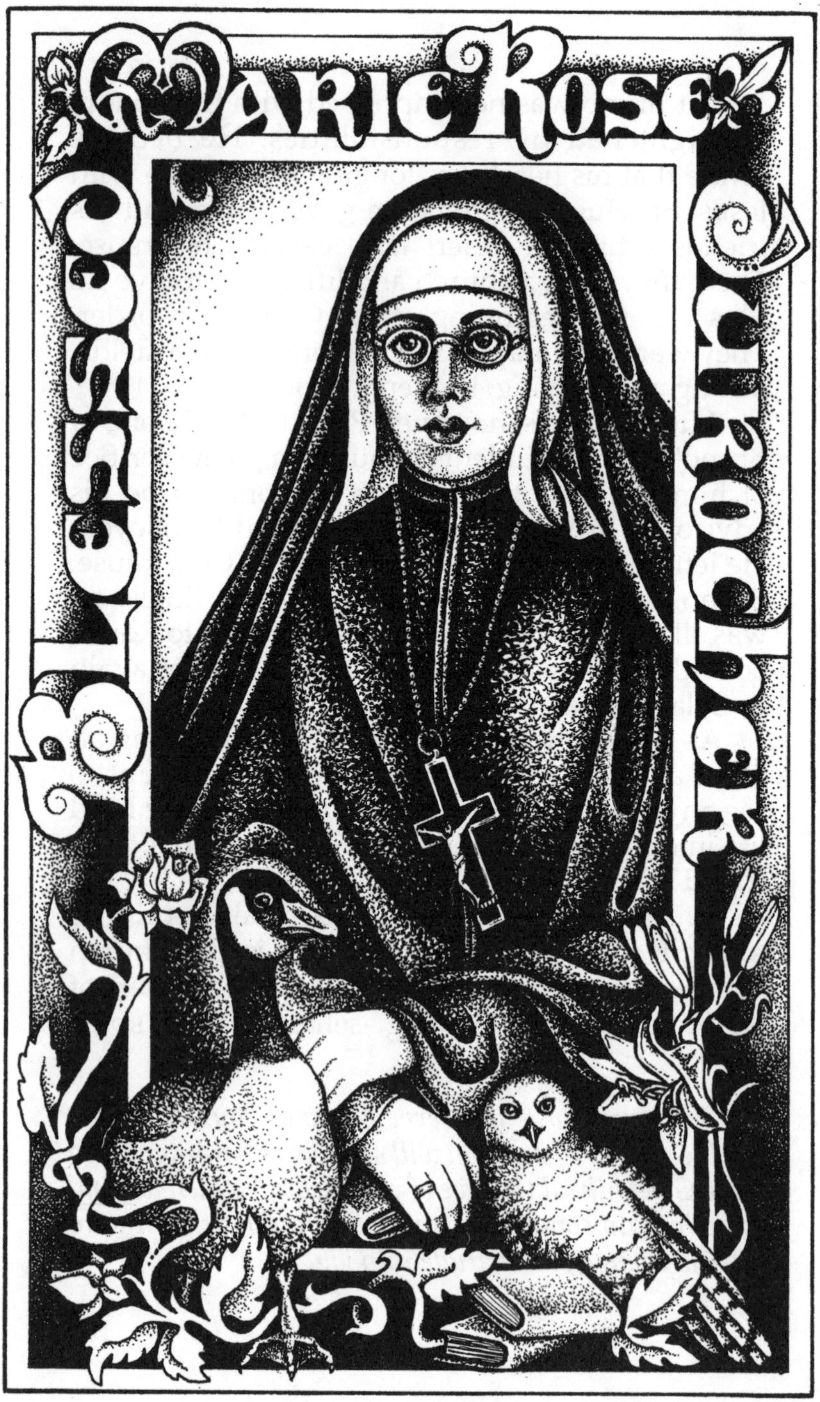
Blessed
Marie Rose
Durocher

BLESSED MARIE ROSE DUROCHER

Eulalie Durocher was born in 1811 in Quebec, Canada. She was the tenth of eleven children. Eulalie's mother died when she was eighteen. Her brother, the pastor of a parish in Beloeil, invited his younger sister to his parish. She became a lay apostle. She took charge of the household duties for her brother, the priest. She also started the first parish sodality in Canada. The thirteen years she was involved in the life of the Church and the parish were preparing her for a special work for God.

In 1843, when Eulalie was thirty-two, the bishop of Montreal asked her to begin a very special mission. Eulalie started a new religious order of women called the Sisters of the Holy Names of Jesus and Mary. Their particular work for Jesus would be to educate the poorest and most neglected children. Eulalie became Mother Marie Rose. Others followed this generous woman. They, too, believed in the importance of educating children for the love of Jesus.

Mother Marie Rose lived only six years after her congregation began. However, she helped her sisters from heaven because the community continued to grow and open new convents. They started a mission in America, too. They went to Oregon in 1859. Today the Sisters of the Holy Names of Jesus and Mary are spread throughout the world.

Mother Marie Rose Durocher was declared "blessed" by Pope John Paul II on May 23, 1982.

We can thank Blessed Marie Rose for the sacrifices she made to educate children. When we are tempted to "take it easy" at school, we can ask her to give us the will power to try our very best.

OCTOBER 7

OUR LADY OF THE ROSARY

It was St. Dominic in the late twelfth and early thirteenth centuries who encouraged everyone to say the Rosary. St. Dominic was greatly saddened by the spread of a terrible heresy called Albigensianism. With the members of his new Order of Preachers, he was trying his best to destroy this dangerous heresy. He begged the Blessed Virgin for help, and it is said that she told him to preach devotion to the Holy Rosary. St. Dominic obeyed and he was very successful in stopping the heresy.

The Holy Rosary is a simple devotion which can be practiced by all people—old and young, learned and unlearned. It can be said anywhere, at any time. While we say the Our Father, ten Hail Marys and Glory to the Father, we think about great moments in the lives of Jesus and Mary. In this way, we grow closer and closer to Jesus and his Blessed Mother. We learn to imitate their holy lives.

Mary is very pleased when we say the Holy Rosary often and well. She used to say it with St. Bernadette when she appeared to her at Lourdes. The three little children of Fatima learned from Mary the power of the Rosary. Mary taught them that the Rosary obtains graces and saves sinners from hell.

A Dominican pope, Pius V, established today's feast. It is to show our gratitude to Mary for a military victory over the Turks at Lepanto on October 7, 1571.

Let us acquire the beautiful habit of saying the Rosary every day.

OCTOBER 8

ST. SIMEON

Holy Simeon lived in the first century. In Luke's Gospel, chapter two, Joseph and Mary bring Jesus to the Temple in Jerusalem. That is where they meet Simeon. The holy man had waited patiently for the Lord to grant him a request: he wanted to live to see the Messiah, the Savior of the world. But he did not know who that person would be, or when and if his prayer would be fulfilled.

The young couple from Nazareth approached him with their baby. He looked into the eyes of the Child and felt a burst of joy in his heart. His eyes glowed. He lifted Jesus into his arms, then held him up and prayed:

"Now, my God, I can die in peace. I have seen with my own eyes the world's salvation. You have prepared this for all your people."

Mary and Joseph looked at one another. They were silently amazed. Then the old man turned to Mary. His eyes became sad as he said softly, "Your own soul will be pierced by the sword." Mary did not understand what this meant, and she prayed to God for courage.

Holy Simeon had received his request from God. He remained in joyful thanksgiving as the couple and their baby left.

We can ask St. Simeon to give us some of his trust in God. We can also ask him to help us be patient when our prayers are not answered as quickly as we desire.

OCTOBER 9

The current Roman calendar lists two saints on October 9. Their stories are briefly presented here one after the other.

ST. DENIS AND COMPANIONS

Denis is very popular in France. In fact, he is considered the patron saint of France. Because he lived at the beginning of Christian history—during the third century—we don't know as much about him as we would like to.

We do know that Denis was born in Italy. He came to France and became the bishop of Paris. He was preaching the Good News of Jesus when he and two companions were martyred. It is believed that his companions were a priest and a deacon. The Christian community cherished the memory of these brave martyrs. At first, they were able to build a little chapel to mark the sight of their death. Later the chapel became the great church of St. Denis.

St. Denis and his companions remind us of the brave men, women and children who have gone before us. They give us the example of their lives. They also remind us that they will help us now if we ask them.

We can pray to St. Denis and his companions today for whatever we need to make us better followers of the Lord Jesus.

ST. JOHN LEONARDI

Born in 1541, John became a pharmacist in Lucca, Italy. When he was twenty-five, John felt the call to become a priest. He began studies and was ordained in 1572. He spent his time teaching children the faith and training catechists. His active ministry also took him to hospitals and prisons. Several young men in Lucca gathered around Father John and helped him with his wonderful works. Eventually, this group was to become a new religious congregation of priests. They were called the Clerks of the Mother of God.

Father Leonardi was given a church as his headquarters in Lucca. His followers took care of the spiritual needs of the people in their new parish. Father Leonardi moved to Rome where his good friend St. Philip Neri lived. St. Philip was his spiritual director. Father Leonardi's work was hard at times because of all the political and spiritual turmoil in Europe. But St. Philip believed in Father Leonardi and in the good his congregation of priests was doing. St. Philip gave him his own house in Rome. It was called "St. William of Charity." With the building came St. Philip's cat. St. John gladly took care of it.

St. John Leonardi and his priests made a strong religious impact on the people of Italy. The order was officially recognized by Pope Clement VIII in 1595. Their founder died of the plague on October 9, 1609, while ministering to victims of the disease. He was proclaimed a saint by Pope Pius XI in 1938.

This saint teaches us to recognize that human beings require spiritual as well as physical care. We can ask St. John Leonardi to remind us to pay attention to the needs of our souls as well as our bodies.

OCTOBER 10

ELEVEN MARTYRS
OF ALMERIA, SPAIN

The Spanish civil war began in 1936. It has been described as a struggle between atheism and belief in God. The particular object of persecution was the Catholic Church. In three years, 12 bishops; 4,184 priests; 2,365 monks and 300 nuns died for the faith. Today we celebrate eleven of those martyrs: two bishops, a diocesan priest, seven Brothers of the Christian Schools, and a young lay woman. The bishops were from Almeria and Gaudix, Spain. The seven Brothers of the Christian Schools were teachers at St. Joseph College in Almeria. Father Pedro Castroverde was a well-known scholar and founder of the Teresian Association. Victoria Diez Molina belonged to the Teresians. She had found a spiritual treasure in the way this group prayed and lived their Christian responsibilities. Victoria was a teacher in a country school and was very active in her parish.

All eleven martyrs chose to die for Jesus rather than give up their Catholic faith. Brother Aurelio Maria, soon to be killed, was the director of St. Joseph College. He said: "What happiness for us if we could shed our blood for the lofty ideal of Christian education. Let us double our fervor so to become worthy of such an honor." Bishop Medina of Gaudix said: "We have done nothing to deserve

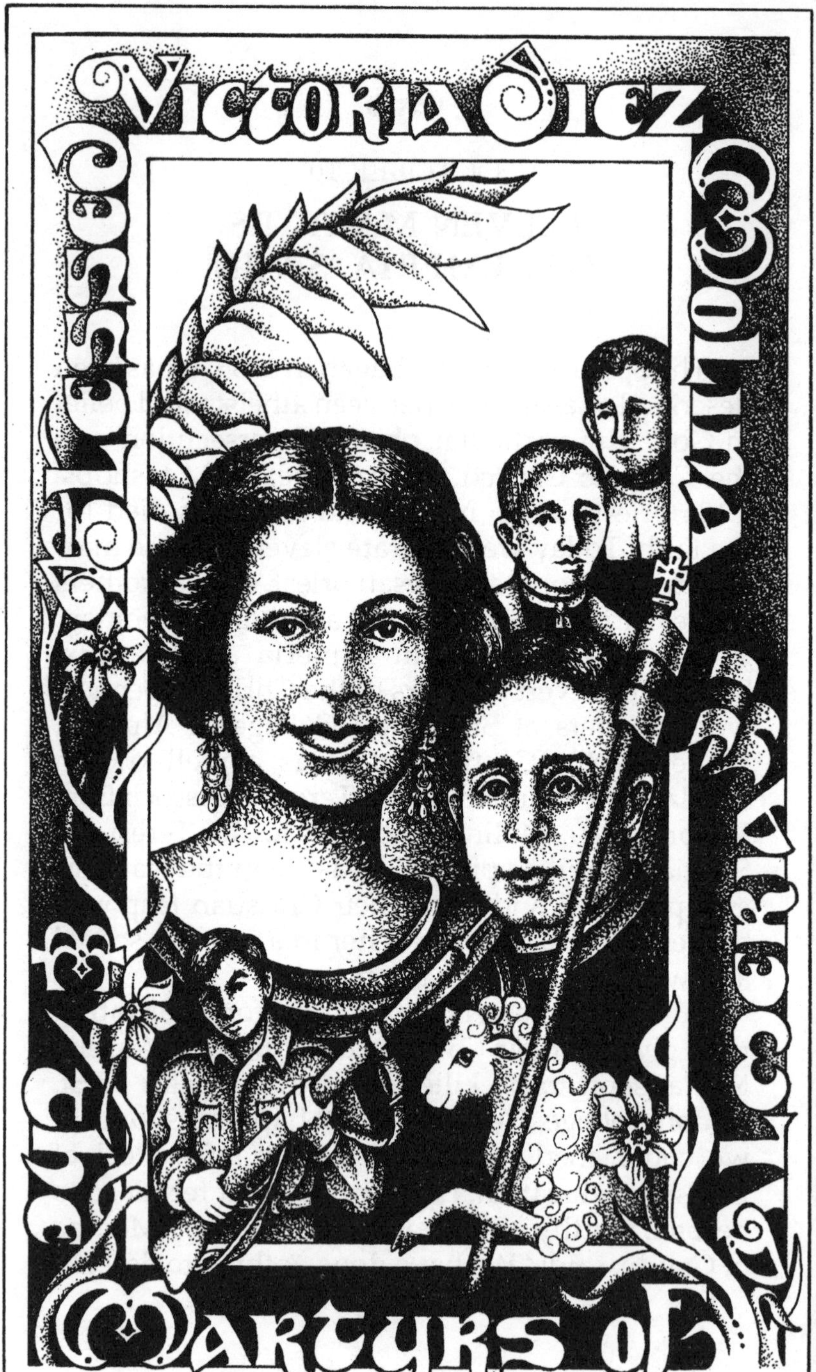

Blessed
Victoria Diez
Martyrs of

death. But I forgive you so that the Lord will also forgive us. May our blood be the last shed in Almeria." Bishop Ventaja of Almeria had many opportunities to flee the country. He chose instead to remain with his suffering people, his suffering Church. Father Castroverde, the Teresian founder, wrote in his diary: "Lord, may I think what you want me to think. May I desire what you want me to desire. May I speak as you want me to speak. May I work as you want me to work." He was killed on July 28, 1936.

Victoria Molina was jailed on August 11, 1936. She and seventeen others were led to an abandoned mine shaft and to their death. Victoria comforted the others and said: "Come on, our reward is waiting for us." Her last words were: "Long live Christ the King."

Pope John Paul II proclaimed these martyrs "blessed" on October 10, 1993.

We can ask these eleven heroes of God to give us their courage. We could make the prayer of Blessed Pedro Castroverde our own:

Lord, may I think what you want me to think. May I desire what you want me to desire. May I speak as you want me to speak. May I work as you want me to work. Amen.

OCTOBER 11

ST. KENNETH

This saint, who is sometimes called St. Canice or Kenny, lived in the sixth century. He was born in Ireland and is famous in both Ireland and Scotland. His father was a bard, that is, a professional singer of ballads and stories in song. As a young man, Kenneth went to Wales to study for the priesthood. St. Cadoc was his teacher. After he became a priest, he went to visit Rome. He then returned to Ireland to study at the school of St. Finnian. Kenneth became good friends with three other Irish saints—Kieran, Comgall and Columba.

After preaching throughout Ireland, St. Kenneth went with St. Columba to Scotland on a mission to the pagan King Brude. When this king angrily seized his sword to strike the two missionaries, it is said that St. Kenneth made the sign of the cross, and a miracle took place. The king's hand was suddenly paralyzed, and the saints were saved. St. Kenneth and St. Columba were always close friends. Once Columba was sailing with some companions. Kenneth was far away in his monastery in Ireland. Suddenly he became aware that Columba was in great danger at sea. He jumped up from the dinner table and ran to church to pray for his beloved friend. Out at sea, Columba cried to his frightened companions: "Don't be afraid! God will listen to Kenneth. Right now he is running to church with only one shoe on to pray for us!" And as he said, they were saved.

St. Kenneth started several monasteries and converted many nonbelievers. He became famous for his zealous preaching of the Gospel. Even more, he became well-known for the perfect way in which he himself practiced the teachings of Jesus.

St. Kenneth knew how to make the best of a situation. His good humor won him many friends and helpers in preaching the Good News. We can ask St. Kenneth to show us how to be as good and cheerful a friend as he was.

OCTOBER 12

ST. FELIX AND ST. CYPRIAN

Felix and Cyprian were African bishops who lived in the fifth century. They suffered with over 4,900 martyrs in the terrible persecution by the Vandals. Huneric, the Vandal king, drove these Christians into exile in the Libyan desert. They were treated with great cruelty by the Moors.

A holy bishop named Victor used to try to help the poor Christians who had been shut up in a horrible prison. They were packed in without sufficient air or light. He wrote the story of their courage and their sufferings. Bishop Victor says that when they were ordered into exile in the terrible desert, they came out of that prison singing hymns. Other Christians burst into tears at the sight of their great courage. Even women and children went with them to exile and death. The story is told of Bishop St. Felix. He was so old and so crippled that someone said to the Vandal king: "You might just as well leave him here to die." But King Huneric cruelly answered, "If he cannot ride a horse, he can be dragged by oxen." In the end, they decided to tie the brave old bishop to a donkey and he was carried off to die in the desert.

We also celebrate St. Cyprian. This bishop lived two centuries after St. Cyprian of Carthage who is honored on September 16. Today's Cyprian risked his own life to take care of as many prisoners as he could. He spent all his time and strength, plus everything he owned, to assist them. At last, he, too, was arrested and sent into exile. There he also died a martyr from the cruel treatment reserved for Christians.

The martyrs gave up all they had, even life itself, to keep their faith in God. We can ask today's martyrs for the gift of their joyful generosity.

ST. EDWARD

King St. Edward was one of the best loved of all the English kings. He lived in the eleventh century. Because of enemies in his own country, he had to live in Normandy, France, from the time he was ten until he was forty. However, when he came back to rule, all the people welcomed him with great joy.

St. Edward was a tall, well-built man, but he was never healthy. Still he was able to rule his country well and keep peace most of the time. This was because he trusted in God and held firm when necessary. King Edward went to daily Mass. He was a gentle, kind man who never spoke sternly. To poor people and foreigners, he showed special charity. He also helped monks in every way he could. It was his justice to everyone and his love for God's Church that made St. Edward so popular with the English people. They would cheer him as he rode out of the castle.

Although he was a king with great power, St. Edward showed his honesty by the way he kept his word—to God and to people. While he was still living in Normandy, he had made a promise to God. He said that if his family would see better times, he would go on a pilgrimage to St. Peter's tomb in Rome. After he was made king, he wanted to keep his vow. But the nobles knew that there would be no one to keep the peace among the warlike people in the land. So, although they admired his devotion, they did not want him to go. The whole matter was brought to the pope, St. Leo IX. He decided that the king could stay home. He said that King Edward was to give to the poor the money he would have spent on the trip. He also was to build or repair a monastery in honor of St. Peter. Obediently, the king carried out the pope's decision. He died in 1066 and was buried in the marvelous monastery he had rebuilt. He was proclaimed a saint by Pope Alexander III in 1161.

St. Edward teaches with his life that money and power are gifts from God. They are to be used responsibly. We can ask St. Edward to bless world leaders with his values so that their people can live peaceful, joyful lives.

OCTOBER 14

ST. CALLISTUS I

This great pope and martyr lived in the first part of the third century. He was once a young slave in Rome, who got into serious trouble. His master, a Christian, had put him in charge of a bank. Somehow, Callistus lost the money deposited with him by other Christians. In fear, he ran away from Rome. He was caught, after jumping into the sea to try to get away. His sentence was a terrible one: he was chained and put to hard labor in a mill.

From this punishment Callistus was released, only because his creditors hoped he could get some of their money back. But once again he was arrested, this time for having gotten into a fight. He was sent to the mines of Sardinia. When the emperor freed all the Christians who had been condemned to those mines, Callistus was freed, too. From that time on, things began to go better for him.

Pope St. Zephrinus came to know and trust the freed slave. He placed him in charge of the public Christian cemetery in Rome. This cemetery is now named after St. Callistus himself. Many popes were buried in it. Callistus proved himself worthy of the pope's confidence in him. St. Zephrinus not only ordained him a priest, but also made him his friend and advisor.

Later on, St. Callistus himself became pope. Some people complained because he showed too much mercy to sinners. However, the holy pope ruled that even murderers could be admitted to communion after they had done penance for their sin. This great pope always defended the true doctrine of Jesus. He ended his life in 222 with a glorious martyrdom.

Fear can lead us to run away from the responsibility of our words and actions. We can ask St. Callistus for courage to admit and make up for our mistakes.

ST. TERESA OF AVILA

Teresa was born in Avila, Spain, on March 28, 1515. As a little girl in her parents' rich home, Teresa and her brother Rodrigo loved to read the lives of the saints and martyrs. It seemed to them that the martyrs got to heaven an easy way. The two children set out secretly to go to the land of the Moors. As they walked along, they prayed that they might die for Christ. But they had not gotten far when they met an uncle. He took them back to their worried mother at once. Next the children decided to be hermits in their garden. This didn't work out either. They could not get enough stones together to build their huts.

St. Teresa herself wrote down these amusing stories of her childhood. The fact is that when she grew to be a teenager, however, she changed. Teresa read so many novels and foolish romances that she lost much of her love for prayer. She began to think more of dressing up to look pretty. But after she recovered from a bad illness, Teresa read a book about the great St. Jerome. Then and there, she made up her mind to become a bride of Christ. As a nun, Teresa often found it hard to pray. Besides that, she had poor health.

Teresa wasted time every day in long, foolish conversations. But one day, in front of a picture of Jesus, she felt great sorrow that she did not love

God more. She started then to live for Jesus alone, no matter what sacrifice had to be made. In return for her love, the Lord gave St. Teresa the privilege of hearing him talk to her. She learned to pray in a marvelous way, too. St. Teresa of Avila is famous for having opened new Carmelite convents. These convents were filled with sisters who wanted to live holy lives. They made many sacrifices for Jesus. Teresa herself gave them the example. She prayed with great love and worked hard at the convent tasks.

St. Teresa was a great leader and true lover of Jesus and his Church. She died in 1582 and was proclaimed a saint by Pope Gregory XV in 1622.

She was declared a Doctor of the Church by Pope Paul VI in 1970.

When we ever need a little "spiritual push" to pray at Mass with more love, we can ask St. Teresa. We can ask her to help us keep our minds on our prayers. She will also show us how to love St. Joseph as she did.

OCTOBER 16

ST. MARGARET MARY

Margaret Mary lived in the seventeenth century. She is the famous French nun to whom Jesus showed his Sacred Heart. As a child, she was a happy little girl who loved the nuns at school. But when she was eleven, she became very sick. It was four years before she was well again. Her father had died, and an aunt had moved into their home. This aunt and her husband made Margaret Mary and her mother suffer very much. Almost every day, the teenager would hide in the garden to cry and pray. What hurt her most was seeing her mother get hurt.

Yet Margaret Mary grew to love good times. A few years later, she was considering marriage. Her mother wanted her to marry and so did her relatives. They were worried about her, especially when she brought beggar children into the garden to try to teach them. Margaret Mary hesitated a while, neither marrying nor entering the convent. At last she decided on the convent.

She joined the Visitation sisters and was a kind, humble sister. Often she made others impatient since she was slow and clumsy. But she was dear to Jesus. He began to appear to St. Margaret Mary to show her how much he loves us all. Jesus wanted her to spread devotion to his Sacred Heart. It was a very hard thing to do. Many people thought Margaret Mary had not really seen Jesus at all. Some were angry with her for trying to spread the new devotion. This brought her great suffering. Yet she did her best to carry out the Lord's wish. Jesus blessed her hard work and pain. Today, this wonderful devotion to the Sacred Heart is practiced all over the world.

Our Lord made great promises to St. Margaret Mary for those who are devoted to his most Sacred Heart. Some of these promises are: "I will comfort them in all their afflictions. I will establish peace in their homes. I will bestow abundant blessings on all their undertakings. I will bless every place where a picture of my Heart shall be displayed and honored." The greatest promise Jesus made is this: "My divine Heart shall be the safe refuge in the last moment to all those who receive Holy Communion on the First Friday for nine months in a row." We can ask St. Margaret Mary to help us understand the importance of devotion to the Sacred Heart of Jesus.

ST. IGNATIUS OF ANTIOCH

St. Ignatius of Antioch has been well-known since earliest times. He was born in the year 50. St. Jerome and St. John Chrysostom both thought of his tomb as near the city gates of Antioch. Ignatius was the third bishop of Antioch. This is the city where St. Peter labored before he moved to Rome. It is also the city where followers of Jesus were first called Christians. Ignatius was condemned to death during the reign of Emperor Trajan. He was led from Antioch to the center of Roman cruelty— the amphitheater.

Although he journeyed to Rome under military guard, Ignatius stopped in Smyrna and Troas. From each of those cities, he wrote letters to the Christian communities. In this way, he used the same methods of preaching the Good News as the great St. Paul. One of the letters Ignatius wrote from Troas was to St. Polycarp, a fellow bishop, who is also a martyr. We celebrate his feast on February 23.

When the beloved Ignatius arrived in Rome, he joined the brave Christians who waited in prisons. The day came when the bishop was pushed out into the amphitheater. Two fierce lions devoured him. He left the beautiful witness of Christian life and his letters. St. Ignatius died around 107.

The next time we feel overwhelmed by an unpleasant situation, we can go to St. Ignatius of Antioch. He will show us how to turn problems into opportunities, the way he did.

OCTOBER 18

ST. LUKE

It is generally believed that Luke was a gentile doctor. He was a good, kind man who came to know the Lord from the great apostle Paul. After he had become a Christian, he went everywhere with Paul. Luke was a great help to him in spreading the faith. The Bible calls Luke "the beloved physician."

St. Luke is the author of two books in the Bible: the Gospel of Luke and the Acts of the Apostles.

Although he did not meet Jesus while the Lord was on this earth, he wanted to write about him for new converts. So he talked to those who had known Jesus. He wrote down all that they had seen the Lord do and heard him say. It is believed that Luke learned some important information from the Blessed Virgin Mary herself. Mary would have been the person who could describe the details of the angel Gabriel's appearance to her at the Annunciation. Mary could have best told about the birth of Jesus in Bethlehem and the flight of the Holy Family into Egypt.

Luke also wrote the story of how the apostles began to teach the message of Jesus after he went back to heaven. It is in Luke's book, The Acts of the Apostles, that we learn how the Church began to grow and spread.

St. Luke is the patron saint of doctors. We are not sure when or where Luke died. He is one of the four evangelists, or Gospel writers.

Luke's Gospel speaks especially of God's mercy for people who are sorry for their sins. Sometimes we become afraid because of our sins and mistakes. We can ask St. Luke to show us how to have confidence in the merciful Jesus, as he did.

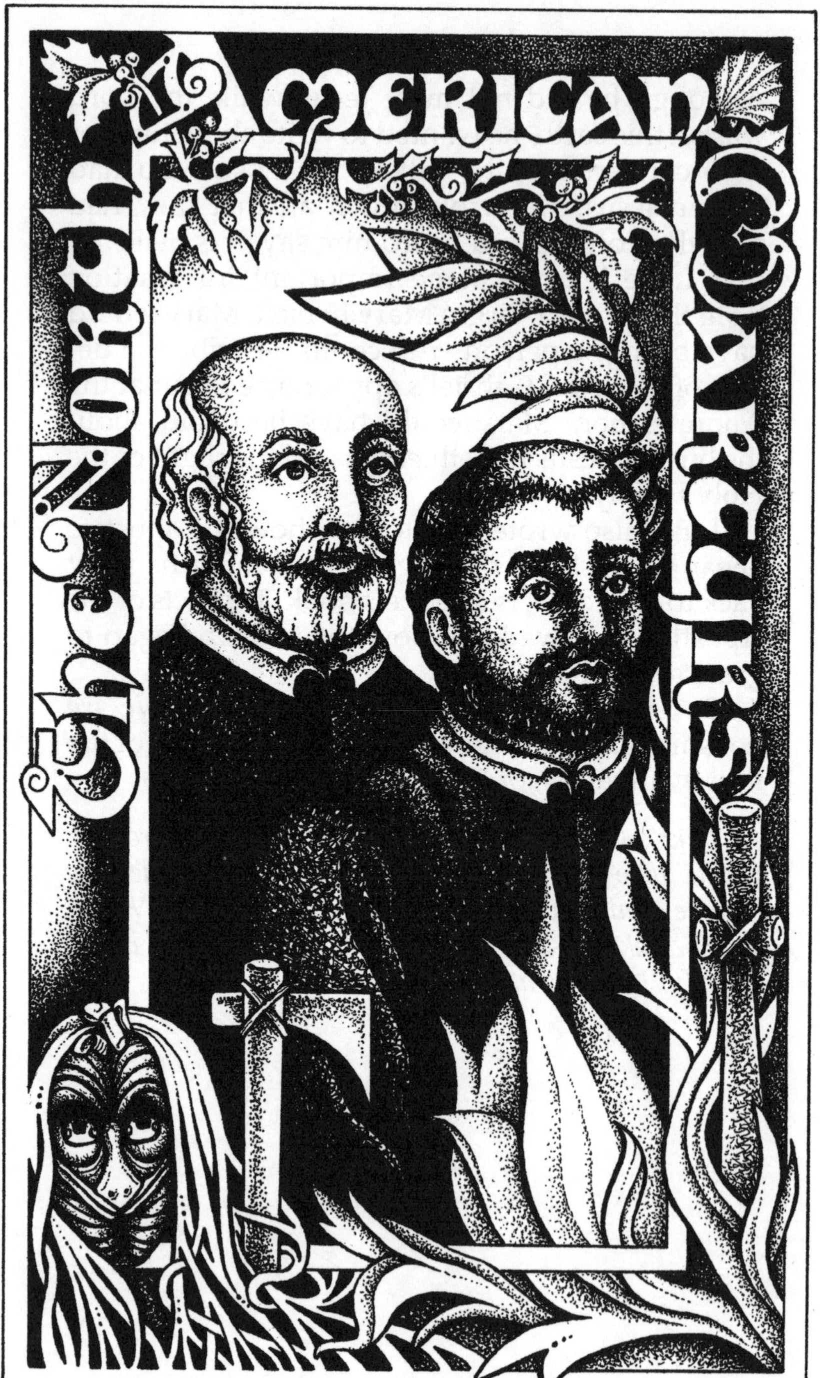
The North
American
Martyrs

ST. ISAAC JOGUES,
ST. JOHN DE BREBEUF
AND COMPANIONS
THE NORTH AMERICAN MARTYRS

Over three hundred years ago, six Jesuit priests and two holy laymen, all from France, died as martyrs here in North America. These eight men were martyred between 1642 and 1649. They were a group of the bravest and most daring missionaries in the New World. They risked everything they had to bring Christ to the native people. After much hard work, they converted many of the Huron tribe. But the Iroquois, bitter enemies of the Hurons, put them all to death.

St. John de Brebeuf had tuberculosis. He was so sick in France that he could not even teach many classes. Yet he became a marvelous, valiant apostle. His courage amazed the fierce Iroquois as they tortured him to death. St. Isaac Jogues was tortured by the Mohawks, but was freed by the Dutch. He went back to France, but as soon as he could, he returned to North America. Father Jogues was killed with a tomahawk by the Bear Clan of the Mohawks. St. Anthony Daniel had just finished celebrating Mass for his Huron converts when the Iroquois attacked the village. The Christian Indians begged him to try to escape. But Father Daniel stayed. He wanted to baptize all those who were crying to him for Baptism before they would be killed. The Iroquois burned him to death in his little chapel. St. Gabriel Lallemont was tortured to death with St. John de Brebeuf. St. Charles Garnier and St. Noel Chabenel were both killed with tomahawks. St. Charles was first shot by an Iroquois musket during a surprise attack, but he still tried to crawl to help a dying man. He was killed by a hatchet blow.

Father Chabenel had found life very hard, but had made a vow to stay in North America. He was killed by a Huron traitor. The two lay helpers, Rene Goupil and John Lalande, were both killed with tomahawks. So it was that these heroes of Christ gave their lives for the native people of North America. After their death, new missionaries were able to convert almost every tribe that the martyrs had known. These brave men, often called the North American martyrs, were proclaimed saints in 1931 by Pope Pius XI.

Many sins committed today offend the dignity of human beings. We can ask these martyrs to share with us their great love and respect for people. We can ask them to give us their great "missionary hearts."

ST. PAUL OF THE CROSS

Paul Danei of Ovada, Italy, was born into a family of merchants in 1694. He was a good Christian and practiced his faith. When he was nineteen, Paul decided to become a soldier. After a year he left the army. During the summer of 1720 Paul had some kind of a spiritual experience. He had three visions of starting a new religious order. He couldn't imagine what was happening, so he went to his bishop for guidance. The bishop investigated and believed that the visions were real. He told Paul to go ahead with his special call. He should do what he was being told in the visions to do.

Paul spent forty days in prayer and penance. During that time he wrote a rule that he and the followers of his new congregation could base their style of life on. Paul was joined by his brother John and two other young men. Paul and John were ordained priests by Pope Benedict XIII in 1727.

Ten years later, the first Passionist monastery was started. Pope Clement XIV approved the new order. He also approved the rule a short time later. Besides the three vows of poverty, chastity and obedience, Paul of the Cross added a fourth vow: devotion to the passion of Christ. By 1747, the Passionists had three monasteries. They were preaching parish retreats throughout Italy.

When he died in 1775, Paul of the Cross was starting a congregation of Passionist nuns. He was proclaimed a saint by Pope Pius IX in 1867.

We all need help when it comes to focusing our minds on spiritual things. We will profit by thinking about the passion and death of Jesus. We can thank the Lord for all that he suffered for us. That is what Paul of the Cross and his religious order do. We can ask St. Paul of the Cross to help us deepen our appreciation for the sufferings of Jesus.

ST. HILARION

Hilarion lived in the fourth century. He was an unbelieving teenager when he left his home in Palestine. He was on his way to Egypt to go to school. There he learned about the Christian faith, and soon he was baptized. Hilarion was only about fifteen at the time. His conversion started him out on a glorious journey leading him closer to God. Before long, he was off to visit the famous St. Anthony in the desert. (We celebrate his feast on January 17.) Hilarion wanted to be alone to serve Jesus, whom he had just come to love.

Hilarion stayed two months with St. Anthony, but it was not quiet enough there for him. Many people came to St. Anthony for help. Hilarion could not find the peace he was looking for, so he left. After giving everything he had to the poor, he went into the wilderness to live as a hermit.

Hilarion had to battle many temptations. At times it seemed to him as if none of his prayers were heard at all. Yet he did not let these temptations stop him from praying even harder.

After twenty years in the desert, the holy man worked his first miracle. Soon many people began coming to his hut to beg his help. Several men asked him to let them stay with him to learn from him how to pray and do penance. In his great love for God and people, the saint invited them to stay. But finally, when he was sixty-five, he began to travel. He went from one country to another in search of peace and quiet. However, the fame of his miracles of mercy always brought crowds of visitors. A few years before his death in 371, Hilarian at last felt that he was truly alone with God. He was eighty years old when he died.

When we think that people and circumstances get in the way of our relationship with God, we can pray to St. Hilarion. He will show us how to find the Lord, even in the midst of noise and confusion.

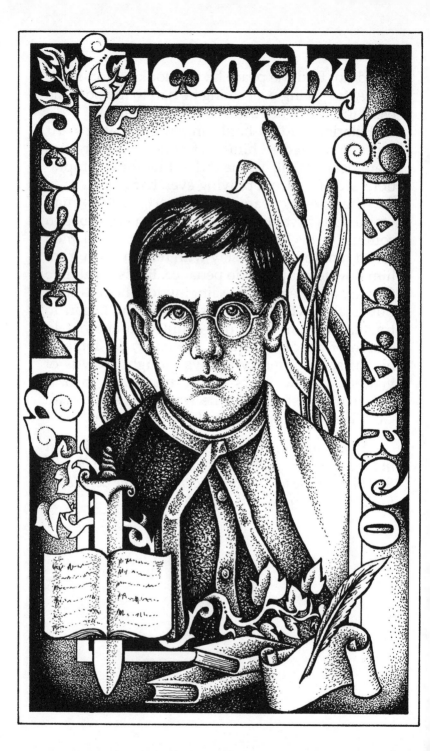

BLESSED TIMOTHY GIACCARDO

Joseph Giaccardo was born on June 13, 1896, in Narzole, Italy. His parents were hard-working farmers. Joseph acquired good habits from them. They loved their Catholic faith, which he learned from them. Joseph prayed to Jesus in the Eucharist and to Mary. He had a little statue of Mary on a ledge in his room.

Joseph became a regular Mass server. That is how he met a young priest who came to help at St. Bernard's church. The priest was about to begin a wonderful new religious order, the Society of St. Paul. His name was Father James Alberione. Joseph liked him very much. Father Alberione was impressed with Joseph, too. He guided Joseph in the spiritual life. The boy entered the seminary in Alba to study for the priesthood. In 1917, though still a seminarian, Joseph asked his bishop for permission to leave the seminary. He wanted to join Father Alberione's new order. The bishop reluctantly permitted Joseph to enter the Society of St. Paul. Joseph professed his vows in 1920. He chose the name "Timothy" after the best-loved disciple of St. Paul. Father Timothy was ordained two years later, the first priest in Father Alberione's new congregation. The order had just been started in 1914.

Father Timothy's particular vocation as a Pauline priest was to be a media apostle. He wrote, edited, printed and distributed the Word of God. He performed many responsible tasks with courage and humility. Some people did not understand the apostolate of the Society of St. Paul and the Daughters of St. Paul. They wondered how priests, brothers and sisters could be publishers. How could they use media as their tools for communicating the Good News? Father Timothy helped people understand the marvelous vocation of the Paulines. He also was a great teacher of the priests and religious who were called to this new apostolate. He served the Lord in northern Italy and in Rome. He became Father Alberione's closest associate. In fact, Father Alberione called Blessed Timothy "most faithful of the faithful." But he was not going to be the successor of the Pauline Founder, as Father Alberione had hoped. Father Timothy became very ill with leukemia. He died on January 24, 1948. He was proclaimed "blessed" by Pope John Paul II on October 22, 1990.

We can ask Blessed Timothy to inspire us to chose media wisely. We can pray:

Blessed Timothy, teach me to use media wisely. Teach me to live wisely as you did. Teach me to love the Word of God and the Eucharist as you did. Teach me to love Mary as you did. Amen.

OCTOBER 23

ST. JOHN CAPISTRANO

St. John Capistrano was born in Italy in 1386. He was a lawyer and governor of the city of Perugia. When enemies of the city threw John into prison, he started to think about the real meaning of life. John's political enemies were not in a hurry to release him. He had plenty of time to realize that what mattered most was the salvation of his soul. So when he was miraculously set free, John entered a Franciscan monastery. He was thirty at the time. For John, life as a poor friar was a big change. He had to sacrifice his independence for the love of Jesus. And he tried with all his heart to do this.

After he became a priest, John was sent out to preach. He and his former novice master, St. Bernardine of Siena, spread devotion to the Holy Name of Jesus everywhere. John preached throughout Europe for forty years. All who heard him were moved to love and serve the Lord better.

An outstanding moment in the life of this saint came at the battle of Belgrade. The Turks had made up their minds to conquer Europe and to wipe out the Church of Jesus. The pope sent St. John Capistrano to all the Christian kings of Europe to beg them to unite to fight the mighty Turkish army. The kings obeyed this poor, barefoot friar. He stirred up their love of God and their courage with his fiery words. But even though a big army of Christians came to fight Mohammed II and his Turks, it looked as though they would lose. The enemy army was much bigger. Then it was that the saint himself, though he was seventy years old, ran to the front lines and encouraged the men to keep fighting. Holding his crucifix up high, this thin, small old man kept crying, "Victory, Jesus, victory!" And the Christian soldiers felt full of more courage than ever. They fought until the enemy ran away in fear.

St. John Capistrano died a short time later, on October 23, 1456. He was proclaimed a saint in 1724.

Just one person can do great things: the person who is on God's side. We can ask St. John Capistrano to share with us some of his enthusiasm and courage to do what is right.

OCTOBER 24

ST. ANTHONY CLARET

Anthony was born in Spain in 1807. It was the same year that Napoleon invaded the country. Perhaps that was a "hint" of the exciting events that would follow Anthony through life. He became a priest in 1835 and was assigned to his home parish. Later he went to Rome and worked to help the missions. He joined the Jesuits as a novice, but his health failed. He returned to Spain and became a pastor. Father Anthony knew that the whole world was a mission field. He had the heart of a missionary. He was a dedicated preacher in his parish. He gave conferences to priests. Father Anthony was convinced of the power of the printed word. He wrote at least 150 books. His most well-known book, *The Right Way*, has reached millions of people.

Some people did not understand the value of Father Anthony's initiatives. His success and his zeal threatened them. Perhaps the opposition was permitted by the Lord so that this energetic priest could visit the Canary Islands in 1848. He spent a year there preaching the Good News. Then he returned to Catalonia, Spain, and his preaching ministry there. In 1849, Anthony started a new religious order called the Missionary Sons of the Immaculate Heart of Mary. They are known as Claretians.

Queen Isabella II of Spain thought highly of St. Anthony. She suggested that he was the best person to become archbishop of Santiago, Cuba. His apostolate in Cuba turned out to be an exciting seven years. Archbishop Anthony visited parishes, speaking out against social evils, especially slavery. He blessed marriages and baptized children. He was a reformer and had enemies. He received death threats often but did not stop his wonderful work until he was recalled to Spain in 1857.

During Anthony's priesthood he was head of a seminary in Madrid. He established the school of St. Michael to foster arts and literature and even tried to start a school of agriculture. He went to Rome to help prepare for the First Vatican Council in 1869 and died in 1870. St. Anthony Mary Claret was declared a saint by Pope Pius XII in 1950.

We can ask St. Anthony Claret to give us a missionary heart. We can pray for people all over the world, especially those who are suffering and poor. We can also help the missions by giving some of our spending money to the missions.

OCTOBER 25

BLESSED RICHARD GWYN

Richard was a Welshman who lived in the sixteenth century. Queen Elizabeth I ruled England and Wales. Because most people in Wales were still Catholic, the queen and her officials tried to crush the faith by cruel laws. Priests or people who were loyal to the Holy Father were put in prison. They were often tortured and killed. Richard became a Catholic after he had finished college and had become a teacher.

Before long, he was a hunted man. He escaped from jail once and a month later was arrested again. "You will be freed," he was told, "if you will give up the Catholic faith." Blessed Richard absolutely refused. He was brought to a non-Catholic church by force. He upset the preacher's whole sermon by clanking his chains loudly. Furious, the officials put him in the stocks for eight hours, and many came to abuse and insult him.

More time in prison and torture sessions followed. The queen's men wanted him to give them the names of other Catholics, but Richard would not. At his trial, men were paid to lie about him, as one of them admitted. The men on the jury were so dishonest that they asked the judge whom he wanted them to condemn. After Blessed Richard was sentenced to death, his wife and baby were brought to court. "Do not imitate your husband," the poor woman was told. In disgust, she bravely snapped, "If you want more blood, you can take my life with my husband's. If you give more money to your witnesses, they will surely find something to say against me, too."

As Blessed Richard was being martyred, he cried out in terrible pain: "Holy God, what is this?" One of the officials mockingly answered: "An execution of her majesty, the queen." "Jesus, have mercy on me!" exclaimed the martyr. Then he was beheaded. The beautiful religious poems Blessed Richard wrote in prison are still in existence. In them, he begged his countrymen of Wales to be loyal to the Catholic faith. Blessed Richard died a martyr in 1584. He was proclaimed "blessed" by Pope Pius XI in 1929.

We can greatly admire Blessed Richard for his bravery. And we can be amazed by his willingness to suffer for what he believed in. We can ask Blessed Richard to make us as strong in our convictions as he was.

ST. EVARISTUS

St. Evaristus lived in the second century. He was from a Jewish family in Bethlehem. They were living in Greece at the time of their son's birth. Evaristus was brought up in the Jewish religion. His father was so pleased with the boy's virtue and knowledge that he sent him to the best teachers.

Evaristus became a Christian when he grew older. So great was his love for his new faith that he decided to become a priest. At Rome, where he performed his ministry, everyone grew to admire and love him. So it was that when the pope was martyred, Evaristus was chosen to take his place. He felt he was completely unworthy of being pope, but God knew better.

These were times of persecution for the Church. Such bad lies were spread about the Catholic faith that the Romans thought nothing of putting Christians to death. Every man who became pope was almost certain of being arrested. For about eight years, Pope St. Evaristus ruled the Church. His zeal was so great that the number of believers grew larger every day. At last, however, he was captured.

The jailers were amazed to see the joy on the holy old man's face as he was led to prison. St. Evaristus thought himself very privileged to have been found worthy to suffer and die for Jesus. No better gift could have been given him than his martyrdom. Pope St. Evaristus died in 107.

If we find ourselves taking our Catholic faith for granted, we can pray to Pope St. Evaristus. We can ask him to fill our hearts with his great love for Jesus and the Church.

OCTOBER 27

BLESSED CONTARDO FERRINI

Contardo was born in 1859. His father was a teacher of mathematics and physics. Mr. Ferrini began very early to teach his little son his own love for study. As a young man, Contardo could speak many languages besides Italian. He did very well in every school and college he went to. His great love for study and for his Catholic faith made his friends nickname him their own "St. Aloysius." (St. Aloysius Gonzaga was a young Jesuit saint known for the goodness and generosity of his life.) It was Contardo who first started clubs for college students to help them become good Christians.

When he was twenty-one, he was offered a chance to study at the University of Berlin in Germany. It was hard for him to leave his home in Italy, but he was happy to meet devout Catholics at the university. He wrote down in a little book what he felt the first time he received the sacrament of Reconciliation in a foreign land. It thrilled him to realize that the Catholic Church is really the same everywhere a person goes.

By the next year, Contardo was trying to decide whether he should become a priest or a monk, or whether he should marry. He kept asking himself just what he should do. As it turned out, he took a vow to give himself only to God. He lived that vow as a lay person; he never became a priest or brother. He went on teaching and writing. He tried always to become a more perfect Christian. While enjoying his favorite sport of mountain-climbing, he would think of God, the Creator of all the beauty he saw. People noticed that there was something different about Professor Ferrini. Once when he had passed by with his usual warm smile, someone exclaimed, "That man is a saint!"

Contardo Ferrini died of typhoid fever on October 17, 1902. He was only forty-three years old. He was declared "blessed" by Pope Pius XII in 1947.

We can offer prayers for lay apostles so that they may be able to do much good. We pray that they may feel the loving support of God's people who profit from their good example.

ST. SIMON AND ST. JUDE

These two apostles of Jesus are honored on the same day. St. Simon was called "the zealous one" because he had so much devotion to the Jewish law. Once he had been called by the Lord to be an apostle, he gave his heart and his energy to preaching the Gospel. With the other apostles, he received the Holy Spirit on the first Pentecost. Then it is believed that he went to Egypt to preach the faith. Afterward he went to Persia with the apostle St. Jude, and the two of them were martyred there.

St. Jude is sometimes called Thaddeus, which means "the brave one." It was he who asked the Lord a famous question at the Last Supper. Jesus had said: "He who loves me will be loved by my Father, and I will love him and manifest myself to him." And St. Jude wanted to know: "Lord, how is it that you are about to manifest yourself to us and not to the world?" Jesus gave him the answer: "If anyone love me, he will keep my word, and my Father will love him, and we will come to him and make our abode with him."

St. Jude is sometimes called the saint of "desperate or impossible cases." People pray to him when things seem hopeless. Often God answers their prayers through the intercession of this beloved apostle.

These two apostles had very different personalities, but each was greatly loved by the Lord. We can ask St. Simon and St. Jude to show us how to accept ourselves and use our gifts for the spread of Jesus' work.

OCTOBER 29

ST. NARCISSUS

Narcissus lived in the second and early part of the third centuries. He was an old man when he was made bishop of Jerusalem. Narcissus was an excellent bishop. Everyone admired his virtues—everyone except people who chose to live evil lives. Three enemies of the saint accused him of a terrible crime. One said: "May I die by fire if it is not true!" The second said: "May I be wasted away by leprosy if it is not true." The third said: "May I be struck blind if it is not true." Yet no one believed their lie. The people had seen Narcissus' good life. They knew the kind of person he was.

Although no one believed the wicked story, Narcissus used it as an excuse to go off to live in the desert. His whole trust was in God, whom he had served so lovingly. And God showed that the story of those men was absolutely false. Narcissus returned to be bishop of Jerusalem, to the great joy of his people. Although he was even older, he seemed to be more zealous than ever. In fact, he seemed stronger than ever, too, for a few years.

Then he became too weak to carry on. He begged God to send him a bishop to help out. Our Lord sent him another saint, Alexander of Cappadocia. With great love and zeal, they ruled the diocese together. Narcissus lived to be over 116 years old. He died in the year 215.

God never abandons those who trust in him. We might worry over what people say about us. That is when we can ask St. Narcissus to teach us his secret for remaining peaceful.

ST. ALPHONSUS RODRIGUEZ

This Spanish saint was born in 1553. He took over the family business of buying and selling wool when he was twenty-three. Three years later, he got married. God sent him and his wife Mary two children. But many sufferings now came to Alphonsus. Business began to be bad, his little daughter died and then his wife. Now this businessman began to think of what God might have in mind for him. He had always been a devout Christian. But from then on, he prayed, did penance, and received the sacraments more than he had ever done.

When he was nearly forty, Alphonsus' son died, too. Despite his great sorrow, he prayed and asked God for the gift of trust. Alphonsus soon asked to be admitted into the Society of Jesus. However, he was told that he must study first. So he went back to school. Little boys made fun of him. He had to beg for his food, because he had given his money to the poor. At last, he was accepted as a brother and was made door-keeper at a Jesuit college.

"That brother is not a man—he is an angel!" his superior said of him years later. Priests who knew him for forty years never heard him say or do anything wrong. His kindness and obedience were known to all. Once, all the chairs in the house, even the chairs from the bedrooms, had been used for a Forty Hours Devotion. By mistake, Brother Alphonsus' chair was not returned until the following year. Yet he never mentioned the fact to anyone.

During his long life, St. Alphonsus had to conquer very strong temptations. Besides that, he had physical pains. Even as he lay dying, he spent a half hour in terrible agony. Then, just before he died, he was filled with peace and joy. He kissed his crucifix and looked lovingly at his fellow religious. He died in 1617 with the name of Jesus on his lips.

St. Alphonsus Rodriguez taught many wonderful lessons with his life. Very important is the way he took whatever events the Lord permitted. He never lost hope. We can go to St. Alphonsus Rodriguez to ask the Lord to give us the gift of trust.

ST. FOILLAN

Foillan was an Irish monk who lived in the seventh century. His two brothers have also been declared saints. They were some of the many zealous Irish apostles. They left their homeland to help other countries that had fewer priests than Ireland. Sts. Foillan, Fursey and Ultan went to England first. They established a monastery in Burgh Castle. From this spot, they did missionary work among the East Angles. When invaders of the land robbed the monastery of everything it had, Sts. Foillan and Ultan decided to preach the Gospel in France. Their other brother, St. Fursey, had already worked as a missionary and had died there.

King Clovis II welcomed the two holy missionaries as he had welcomed their brother before them. Foillan was given land by Blessed Itta and her daughter. St. Gertrude asked him to preach to the nuns of the convent over which she was abbess. He did so, and had great influence on them. He also did missionary work among the people. In fact, St. Foillan is a well-remembered Irish saint in Europe.

One day, after celebrating Mass for St. Gertrude and her nuns, Father Follian set out on a journey with three companions. They were going to see his brother Ultan, who was preaching in another area. While passing through a forest, they were attacked by a band of robbers and killed. Their bodies were not found for about two and a half months. Then St. Gertrude had St. Foillan buried with honor in the abbey he had started.

We all realize that we have to die some day. We can ask St. Foillan to help us in the hour of our death. St. Foillan will show us how to offer up all our sufferings to Jesus.

november

NOVEMBER 1

ALL SAINTS' DAY

This feast day grew out of the love and devotion of God's people. It is so much a part of ourselves to feel gratitude for and to honor the saints. We mean *all* of the women, men and children who have died and are now in heaven.

Some passed through purgatory to be purified for the Lord's presence. They stayed until the moment when they were ready to see God. They are with him now forever. Some saints have been singled out for their own feast day. The Church offers their witness of heroic, joyful lives for Jesus. But there aren't enough days of the year to fit all the countless saints who walked through this life witnessing to Jesus.

Some kept close to the Lord all their lives. Others found him along the way. Some led good lives without major difficulties. Others made big mistakes, but found the Lord on the road of repentance and genuine sorrow.

They made it! We celebrate their journey that led to eternal happiness with God. We celebrate our own family members, relatives, neighbors and friends whom we believe to be in heaven.

Today we can rejoice in our hearts with all the saints in heaven. We can make up our own prayer to them, thanking them for the witness of their lives. We can thank them, too, for helping us overcome our difficulties and temptations. We ask them to help us on our own journey through life.

ALL SOULS' DAY

This feast day is one of the most loving celebrations in all the Church's liturgy. It is the day that we especially remember all the faithful departed—those who have passed from this life into the next.

We don't know how long a particular individual who dies spends in purgatory. However, we do know that purgatory is real. Today we stop to remember all who have died. We especially pray for those who were related to us. We pray for those who taught us good things. We pray for those who made sacrifices for us. We pray for those who prayed for us while they were on this earth. We pray for the most forgotten souls. We pray for those who had great responsibilities while they were on earth.

We think of those holy souls in purgatory and we realize that they are saved. Now they wait, being purified, until the moment when they can be with God, face to face.

We can pray for the souls in purgatory and hasten their journey to God.

Eternal rest, grant to them, O Lord, and let perpetual light shine upon them. May they rest in peace. Amen.

NOVEMBER 3

ST. MARTIN DE PORRES

Martin was born in Lima, Peru, in 1579. His father was a knight from Spain. His mother was a freed slave from Panama. His father at first left Martin and his mother and sister alone in Peru. They were very, very poor.

Martin grew up good and devout. He was sent to learn the trade of a barber. He also learned how to cure many diseases according to the practices of those days. Martin's father finally decided to take care of his son's education. However, Martin wanted to give himself to God as a Dominican brother. Brother Martin soon proved to be a wonderful religious. No one was kinder or more obedient or holy. Before long, he began to work miracles, too. He cured so many sick people that everyone in the city of Lima would send for Brother Martin when there was sickness. He would go to them all, blacks and whites alike. He loved all people as his brothers and sisters in Christ. Great sums of money were given to this good, lovable Brother for his charities. People recognized how well he could organize works of charity.

Not even animals were forgotten by this kind-hearted saint. He excused the comings and goings of rats and mice by saying, "The poor little things don't have enough to eat." In his sister's house, he kept a "home for wandering cats and dogs."

Despite his fame in Lima, St. Martin always had a very humble opinion of himself. His name for himself was, in fact, "Brother Broom." Martin died on November 3, 1639. When he died, this beloved saint was carried to his tomb by bishops and noblemen. They wanted to honor the humble and holy brother. He was proclaimed a saint by Pope John XXIII in 1962.

We are all children of God. Our Heavenly Father has no preference when it comes to the color of a person's skin. He looks instead into our hearts. We can ask St. Martin de Porres to give us some of his love for people.

NOVEMBER 4

ST. CHARLES BORROMEO

Charles lived in the sixteenth century. He was the son of a rich Italian count. Like other wealthy young men, he went to the University of Pavia. Unlike many of them, however, he would have nothing to do with sinful activities. He seemed to be a slow student because he was not a good speaker, but he really made good progress.

He was only twenty-three when his uncle, Pope Pius IV, gave him many important duties. Charles managed to handle all his affairs well. He was always afraid that he might stray from God because of the many temptations around him. For this reason, he was careful to deny himself many pleasures and to make the effort to be humble and patient.

As a priest and later the cardinal archbishop of Milan, St. Charles was a model for his people. He gave away great amounts of money to the poor. He had only one shabby cassock (long black habit) to his name. In public, though, he dressed as a cardinal should. He attended with great care to the dignity and respect owed to Church ceremonies. In Milan the people had many bad practices and much superstition. By wise laws, by gentle kindness and by his own marvelous example, St. Charles made his diocese a model for the whole Church. He was never a good speaker—people could barely hear him—yet his words took effect.

When a terrible disease caused many deaths in Milan, Cardinal Borromeo thought of nothing else but caring for his people. He prayed and did penance. He organized crews of attendants and went into debt to feed the hungry. He even had altars set up in the streets. This was for the benefit of the sick who could assist at Mass from their windows.

This great man was never too busy to help simple people. He once stayed with a little shepherd boy until he had taught him the Our Father and the Hail Mary. As he lay dying at the age of forty-six, St. Charles said peacefully, "Behold, I come!" He died on November 3, 1584, and was proclaimed a saint by Pope Paul V in 1610.

If we are tempted to "take it easy," we can say a prayer to St. Charles Borromeo. We can ask him for a generous amount of his energy and willingness to do hard work well.

NOVEMBER 5

ST. BERTILLA

Bertilla lived in the seventh century. The first biography of her life appeared in Latin in the year 800. She was born in Soissons, France. While a teenager, she felt the call to grow closer to God. She began to realize that the life of prayer and sacrifice that she wanted could be found in a monastery. She went to her bishop, St. Ouen, and asked his advice. He encouraged her to follow her calling. Her parents sent her to a monastery of nuns who followed the rule of an Irish monk, St. Columban. When she arrived, she knew that she had found peace. Years passed. Bertilla spent her time praying and doing different tasks. She was especially good at offering hospitality to travelers and the sick who came to the monastery. She also cared for the children who were being educated at the monastery.

St. Bathildis, the wife of King Clovis II, started a new monastery. She asked the abbess at Soissons to send some nuns to begin the community. Bertilla was among those chosen and she was appointed the abbess. She was very surprised, but decided to do the best she could. She knew that the Lord would help her in every way. The community of nuns grew. Queen Bathildis herself became a nun after her husband died. Then, another queen, Hereswitha, widow of the king of the East Angles, became a nun, too. Abbess Bertilla must have been amazed to have two queens in her community. But everyone lived in peace because the queens were as humble as the abbess.

Bertilla lived a long life and ruled the monastery of Chelles for forty-six years. She died around the year 705.

The Lord has a plan for each of us. He offers us some task or path in life. Like St. Bertilla, we have to give Jesus the chance to speak. We have to let him be heard. We can ask St. Bertilla to help us recognize and follow God's will for us.

ST. THEOPHANE VENARD

Even as a youngster this holy French priest dreamed of being a martyr. He went to study for the priesthood. Then he entered a college for missionaries in Paris, France. His family, whom he dearly loved, was greatly saddened to think that after he became a priest, he would leave them. Travel was not what it is today. Theophane realized that the long ocean voyage to the Orient would most probably separate him from his family for the rest of his life.

"My darling sister," he wrote in a letter, "how I cried when I read your letter. Yes, I well knew the sorrow I was going to bring on my family. I think there will be a special sorrow for you, my dear little sister. But don't you think it cost me bloody tears, too? By taking such a step, I knew that I would give all of you great pain. Whoever loved his home more than I do? All my happiness on this earth was centered there. But God, who has united us all in bonds of most tender affection, wanted to draw me from it."

After being ordained a priest, Theophane set out for Hong Kong. He sailed in September, 1852. He studied languages for over a year there. Then he went on to Tongking. Two obstacles were in the way of this zealous missionary: his poor health and a terrible persecution. Yet he struggled bravely on. Often he wrote to tell his beloved sister in France all his adventures and narrow escapes from his persecutors. At last, after bravely serving the many Christians in Tongking, Theophane was captured and chained in a cage for two months.

His gentle ways won even his jailers. He managed to write a letter home in which he said: "All those who surround me are civil and respectful. A good many of them love me. From the great mandarin down to the humblest private soldier, everyone regrets that the laws of the country condemn one to death. I have not been put to the torture like my brethren." But their sympathy did not save his life. After he had been beheaded, crowds rushed to soak handkerchiefs in his blood. He was martyred on February 2, 1861. Father Venard was declared a saint by Pope John Paul II on June 19, 1988. He is one of the martyrs of Vietnam celebrated on November 24.

St. Theophane did not spend a long time in China. The great gift that he gave to the people was his life as a martyr. He teaches us that good example is a wonderful influence on people. We can ask St. Theophane to give us the courage to be witnesses for Jesus with the way we live.

ST. WILLIBRORD

Willibrord was born in England in 658. He was educated for many years at an Irish monastery. Most of his life he was a missionary in lands which today are Germany, Holland, Luxemburg and Denmark. He had long had a great desire to preach the Gospel to the nonbelievers of those countries. At last, his dream came true. With the encouragement of the pope, who made him a bishop, St. Willibrord led many people to accept Christianity. The king of the Franks, Pepin, also cooperated with Willibrord.

One very stubborn king made it hard for the saint. This was Rodbod, king of Upper Friesland. At one time the missionary's ship was driven onto an island which the pagans of Denmark and Friesland (a province in the north Netherlands) considered sacred to their god. No one was permitted to kill any animal on it. They could not eat any vegetable or fruit that grew there, or draw from its spring, unless in complete silence. To show them that their god did not exist, St. Willibrord killed some game to provide food for his companions. He also baptized three persons in the spring. Hearing him pronounce the words, "I baptize you" loudly, the pagans felt sure he would drop dead. Of course, nothing happened. King Rodbod was told of this event and he ordered that one of the Christians should die to "calm the god's anger." So it was that one became a martyr.

After this king died, St. Willibrord eagerly went ahead converting many nonbelievers. Although he was growing very old, nothing could stop this apostle. He was still a fine-looking man, cheerful, wise, devout. He was full of love and concern for people right to the end of his life. Bishop Willibrord died in 739.

There are different kinds of superstitions in our own time. Can you think of some? St. Willibrord is a good saint to pray to for keeping us away from superstitions.

NOVEMBER 8

ST. GODFREY

Godfrey lived in the twelfth century. He received his education from the monks of Mont-Saint-Quentin. Godfrey became a monk and a priest. He was chosen to be abbot of the monastery in Champagne, France. The monastery was run-down and only six monks remained. The monks liked Godfrey. They realized that he was a holy man. They admitted that he could help them find again the joy of a self-sacrificing life. In a short while, the community was fervent and new candidates joined them. The abbey of Champagne became a center of prayer and spiritual joy.

Eventually, their abbot was consecrated an archbishop. He was given the well-known diocese of Rheims, France. He felt bad to leave the small monastery. He knew, though, that the Lord wanted him to reach out to the people of Rheims as well. He still lived like a simple monk. His house was poor but clean. His food was plain. Once in a while, his cook prepared food that seemed to him too fancy. Godfrey would wait until the cook was out on errands. Then he would call in the poor people who lived nearby. He would give them the food to take home to their families.

Archbishop Godfrey suffered because of the abuses in his diocese. Some things going on were very wrong. When Godfrey tried to correct those involved, his corrections were resented at times. One person even tried to kill him. It was then that Godfrey wondered if he was doing more harm than good. But people with good will appreciated and loved him. Before he could resign, he died. It was November, 1115.

Sometimes we find that we try our best to do something well. But it doesn't seem to be appreciated. Then we can ask St. Godfrey to teach us how to trust that God will make it work well.

NOVEMBER 9

ST. THEODORE TIRO

Theodore lived in the third century. He was a new soldier in the Roman army when he was called to die for the faith. Although he was young, he knew how to keep his soul pure. He was a prudent person who considered the devil a real enemy. When his legion had camped for the winter in the country of Pontus, all the soldiers were taking part in services to the pagan gods. Since he was a Christian, he knew that these gods did not exist. So Theodore refused to join in the pagan rites. He was arrested.

"How dare you profess a religion which the emperor punishes with death?" demanded the governor. Without hesitation, the young soldier answered, "I do not know your gods. Jesus Christ, the only Son of God, is my God. If you take my answer as an offense, cut off my tongue. Every part of my body is ready to suffer when God calls for this sacrifice."

The pagan judges let Theodore go this time. Then he was arrested later. The judges first tried to win him with kindness. When that treatment did not work, they tried to frighten him by describing the tortures he would go through. In the end, they turned him over to the torturers.

When the suffering soldier was led back into prison, some said that angels came to comfort him.

After he had been questioned three times, he was finally condemned to death by fire in the year 306. A beautiful church was later built to enshrine his ashes. Great crowds of people began going to it to pray to the martyr.

St. Theodore was noted for his bravery and clean living. We, too, are faced with important choices involving right and wrong.

ST. LEO THE GREAT

St. Leo, a Roman, lived in the fifth century. At the death of Pope Sixtus, he became pope. Those were hard times for the Church. Barbarian armies were attacking Christians in many places. Within the Church, some people were spreading errors about the faith, too. But St. Leo was one of the greatest popes there ever was. He was absolutely unafraid of anything or anyone. He had great trust in the help of the first pope, St. Peter the apostle. He prayed to St. Peter often.

To stop the spread of false teachings, St. Leo explained the true faith with his famous writings. He called a Council to condemn the wrong doctrines. Those who would not give up their mistaken beliefs were put out of the Church. And Pope Leo received back into the Church those who were sorry. He asked people to pray for them.

When a large army of barbarians called Huns came to attack Rome, all the people were filled with fear. They knew that the Huns had already burned many cities. To save Rome, St. Leo rode out to meet the fierce leader, Attila. The only weapon he had was his great trust in God. When they met, something wonderful happened. Attila, the cruel pagan leader, showed the pope great honor. He made a treaty of peace with him. Attila said afterward that he had seen two mighty figures standing by the pope while he spoke. It is believed that they were the great apostles, Peter and Paul. They had been sent by God to protect Pope Leo and the Christians.

Because of his humility and charity, Pope Leo was loved by all. He was pope for twenty-one years. He died on November 10, 461.

We often read that the Church is suffering persecution in some countries around the world. We can ask St. Leo to protect the pope, bishops, priests, religious and lay people. We can ask Pope Leo to help all Catholics be courageous as he was.

ST. MARTIN OF TOURS

This soldier saint lived in the fourth century. He joined the Roman army in Italy when he was only fifteen. Although his parents were pagans, he began to study the Christian religion. Those who study the Christian religion are called catechumens until they are baptized.

One very cold winter day, Martin and his companions came upon a beggar at the gate of the city of Amiens. The man's only clothes were nothing but rags and he was shaking with cold. The other soldiers passed by him, but Martin felt that it was up to him to help the beggar. Having nothing with him, he drew his sword and cut his long cloak in half. Some laughed at his funny appearance as he gave one half to the beggar. Others felt ashamed of their own selfishness. That night, Jesus appeared to Martin. He was wearing the half of the cloak that Martin had given away.

"Martin, still a catechumen, has covered me with this garment," Jesus said. Right after this wonderful event, St. Martin went to be baptized.

A few years later, the saint left the army. He became a disciple of St. Hilary, the bishop of Poitiers, France. Because of his strong opposition to the Arian heretics in various cities, Martin had to go into exile. But he was happy to live in the wilderness with other monks. When the people of Tours asked for him as their bishop, he refused.

The people would not give up, however. They got him to come to the city to visit a sick person. Once he was there, they took him to the church. As bishop of Tours, St. Martin did all he could to rid France of paganism. He prayed, he worked, he preached everywhere.

Our Lord let Martin know when his death was near. As soon as his followers heard of it, they began to weep. They begged him not to leave them. So the saint prayed: "Lord, if your people need me yet, I will not refuse the work. Your will be done." He was still laboring for the Divine Master in a far-off part of his diocese when death finally came in 397. St. Martin's tomb became one of the most famous shrines in all of Europe.

It is so easy to be concerned about our own interests. But, like Martin, we want to be aware of the needs of others too. We can ask St. Martin to share with us his generosity.

NOVEMBER 12

ST. JOSAPHAT

Josaphat was born in the Ukraine and baptized John in 1580. He became a monk in the order of St. Basil and chose the name Basil. He was a self-sacrificing, brave man. Because of his many natural qualities, he was chosen for leadership roles. This would eventually cost him his life.

Josaphat became an apostle of ecumenism. He preached union among the Christian churches of the Ukraine. There were three main categories of Christians: the Latin Church united with the pope, the Orthodox Greek Church and the Greek Catholic Church.

Josaphat became a bishop and took over the diocese of Polotsk in 1617. He spent the next ten years helping the people know and love their Catholic faith better. He organized celebrations of prayer and religion classes. He called clergy meetings and worked with the priests to put into effect rules that helped the people live closer to Jesus.

Archbishop Josaphat had great positive influence on people. He was a dynamic leader. For this, some people feared him. They stirred up a mob against him. Josaphat was murdered. His body was thrown into a local river. Josaphat died on November 12, 1623. He was proclaimed a saint by Pope Pius IX in 1867.

St. Josaphat was a peacemaker and a healer. He wanted to bring people together to live in peace. He believed in stressing what unites people, not what divides them. We can ask St. Josaphat to help us be like him.

ST. FRANCES XAVIER CABRINI

Frances was born on July 15, 1850. As a child growing up in Italy, she dreamed about being a missionary to China. She sailed paper boats down a stream to play her "pretend game." The paper boats were ships taking missionaries to China. And she began giving up candy because in China, she probably wouldn't be able to have any. But when she grew up, Frances was not accepted into the two convents which she asked to join. Her health was not too good. She taught school for a while. Then a priest asked her to help out in a small home for orphans. Things were very hard for Frances because of the lady who ran the house. Yet Frances stuck to the work, and some other generous women joined her. Together they took vows.

At last the bishop told Frances to begin her own congregation of missionary nuns. Without hesitating, Frances started at once. This congregation is called the Missionary Sisters of the Sacred Heart. Before long, it began to grow, first in Italy and then in many other countries. Frances, whom everyone called Mother Cabrini, had always had her heart set on going to China. But it seemed that God wanted her to come to America. When Pope Leo XIII told her, "Go west, not east," the matter was settled. St. Frances Xavier Cabrini sailed for the

251

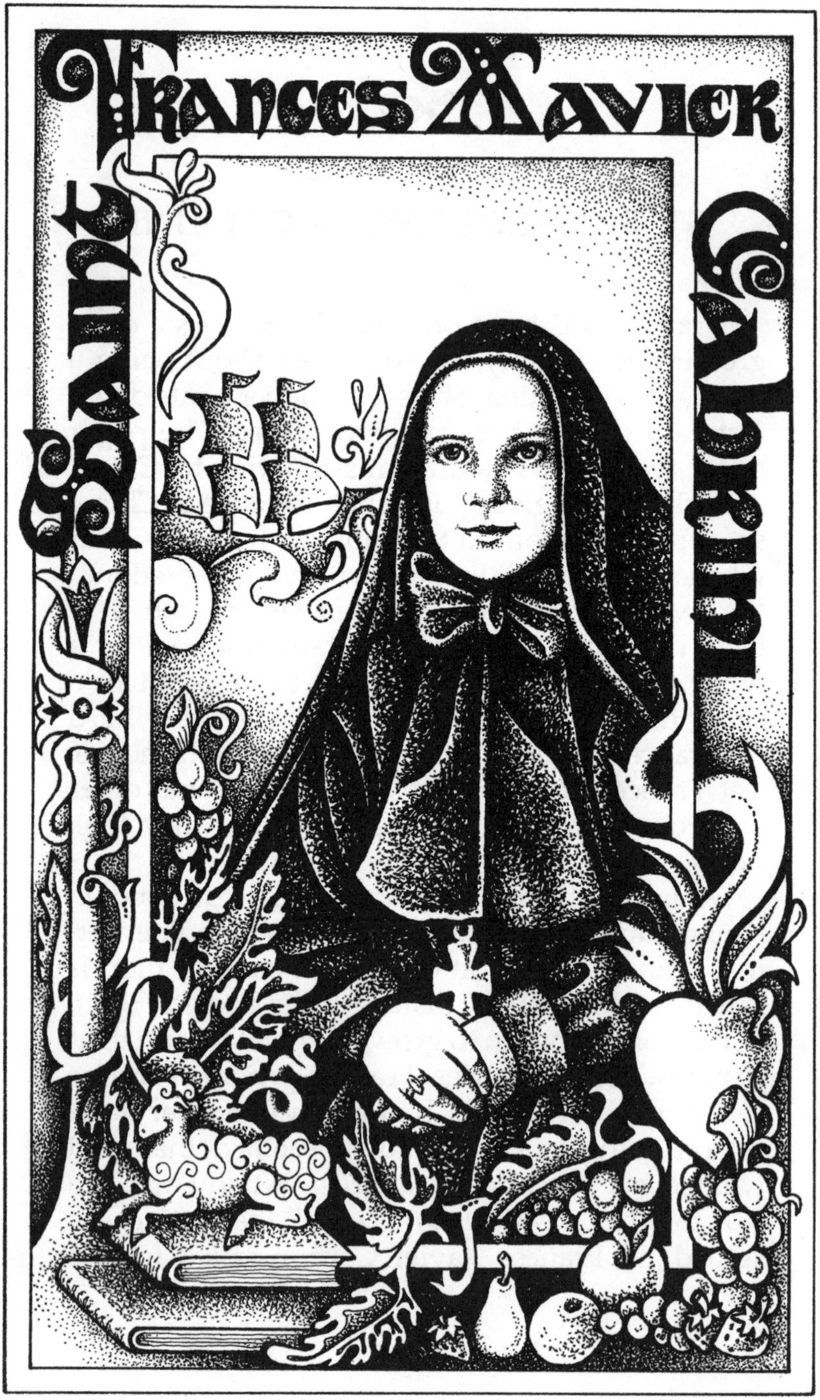
Saint
Frances Xavier
Cabrini

United States and became an American citizen. She especially helped large numbers of Italian immigrants. She was their real mother and friend.

Mother Cabrini and her sisters had a very hard time in the beginning. The archbishop of New York even suggested that they go back to Italy. But Mother Cabrini answered, "Your excellency, the pope sent me here and here I must stay." The archbishop admired her pioneer spirit, and so she and her sisters were permitted to begin their great work for God. Schools, hospitals, and homes for children were opened up in different states. As the years passed, Mother Cabrini made many trips to spread her congregation and its works. There were always difficulties, but she put all her trust in the Sacred Heart. "It is he who is doing everything, not us," she would say.

Mother Cabrini died in Chicago on December 23, 1917. She was proclaimed a saint by Pope Pius XII in 1946.

Where did this frail, sickly woman get the strength to do all that she did? Through prayer. We can ask Mother Cabrini to teach us to value prayer as she did.

NOVEMBER 14

ST. LAWRENCE O'TOOLE

Lawrence was born in Ireland in 1128. He was the son of a chief. When he was only ten years old, a neighboring king made a raid on his father's territory and carried him away. The boy suffered for two years. Then his father forced the king to give him up to the care of a bishop. When he did, Lawrence's father hurried to see his son. He gratefully brought him home.

The chief wanted one of his sons to enter the service of the Church. While he was wondering which one it might be, Lawrence told him with a laugh that he need not wonder anymore. "It is my desire," said Lawrence, "to have for my inheritance the service of God in the Church." So his father took him by the hand and gave him into the care of the bishop. Lawrence became a priest and the abbot of a great monastery. Once food became very scarce in the whole neighborhood of the monastery. The good abbot gave great quantities away to keep the people from starving. He had many problems to handle as head of the monastery, too. Some of the monks criticized him for being too strict. But Lawrence kept right on guiding the community in the way of self-sacrifice, despite the criticism. Then, there was the problem of the robbers and outlaws who lived in the nearby hills. Yet nothing discouraged the fearless Lawrence O'Toole.

He became so famous that before long he was chosen to be archbishop of Dublin. In this new position, he lived as holy a life as ever. Every day, he invited many poor people to be his guests. He helped many others besides. Lawrence dearly loved his people and Ireland, his country, and he did all he could to keep it at peace. Once a madman attacked him as he was going up to the altar to say Mass. He was knocked to the floor unconscious. Yet he came to his senses right away. He had the wound washed at once, and then went right ahead with the Mass.

After years of labor for the Church, St. Lawrence O'Toole became very ill. When he was asked if he wanted to make a will, the holy archbishop smiled. He answered, "God knows that I don't have a penny in the world." He had long ago given everything he had to others, just as he had given himself completely to God. St. Lawrence O'Toole died on November 14, 1180. He was proclaimed a saint by Pope Honorius III in 1225.

St. Lawrence O'Toole reminds us by the way he lived his life that we should be concerned about pleasing God. We can ask St. Lawrence to help us do what is right even if we are criticized for it.

ST. ALBERT THE GREAT

This saint lived in the thirteenth century. He was born in a castle on the Danube River in Swabia (southwest Germany). Albert went to the University of Padua in Italy. There he decided to become a Dominican. His uncle tried to persuade him not to follow his religious vocation. Albert did anyway. He felt that this was what God wanted. His father, the count of Bollstadt, was very angry. The Dominicans thought that he might make Albert come back home. They transferred the novice to a location farther away, but his father did not come after him.

St. Albert loved to study. The natural sciences, especially physics, geography and biology, interested him. He also loved to study his Catholic religion and the Bible. He used to observe the ways of animals and write down what he saw, just as scientists do today. He wrote a great number of books on these subjects. He also wrote on philosophy and was a popular teacher in different schools.

One of St. Albert's pupils was the great St. Thomas Aquinas. It is believed that Albert learned of the death of St. Thomas directly from God. He had guided St. Thomas in beginning his great works in philosophy and theology. He also defended his teachings after Thomas died.

As St. Albert grew older, he became more holy. Before, he had expressed his deep thoughts in his writings. Now he expressed them in his whole way of living for God.

Two years before his death, St. Albert's memory failed him. His end came very peacefully. He was sitting in his chair talking with his fellow Dominicans. St. Albert is the patron saint of students and of the natural sciences.

We can learn from St. Albert how to appreciate and use our minds. Let us say a prayer to St. Albert. We can ask him to help us acquire good learning skills.

NOVEMBER 16

The current Roman calendar lists two saints on November 16. Their stories are briefly presented here one after the other.

ST. MARGARET OF SCOTLAND

Margaret was an English princess born in 1046. She and her mother sailed to Scotland to escape from the king who had conquered their land. King Malcolm of Scotland welcomed them. He fell in love with the beautiful princess. Margaret and Malcolm were married before long.

As queen, Margaret changed her husband and the country for the better. Malcolm was good, but he and his court were very rough. When he saw how wise his wife was, he willingly listened to her good advice. Margaret helped him control his temper and practice the Christian virtues. She made the court beautiful and civilized. The king and queen were wonderful examples because of the way they prayed together and treated each other. They fed crowds of poor people. They tried very hard to imitate Jesus in their own lives.

Margaret was a blessing for all the people of Scotland. Before she came, there was great ignorance. Many people had bad habits that kept them from growing closer to God. Margaret worked hard to obtain good teachers to help the people correct evil practices. She and Malcolm had new churches built. She loved to make the churches beautiful to honor God. In fact, Queen Margaret embroidered some of the priests' vestments herself.

Margaret and Malcolm had six sons and two daughters. They loved all their children very much. The youngest boy became St. David. But Margaret had sorrows, too. In her last illness, she learned that both her husband and her son, Edward, had been killed in battle. They died just four days before Margaret's death. She died on November 16, 1093. Margaret was proclaimed a saint by Pope Innocent IV in 1250.

St. Margaret shows us the importance of doing the right things for the right reasons. Her good example was a genuine reflection of her faith in Jesus. She did not do things right so that she would win praise or be called good. She did things right to please Jesus. We can ask her to help us be the same.

ST. GERTRUDE

Gertrude entered a convent in Saxony when she was very young. Under the care of St. Mechtildis, she grew to be a happy, holy nun. Gertrude was likeable and intelligent. She did very well in Latin studies. In fact, she did not like the study of religion as well as her other subjects at first. But when she was twenty-six, Jesus appeared to her. He told her that from now on, she would think only of loving him and trying to become holy. Now she began to study the Bible with deep delight. She became very learned in our holy religion.

Jesus appeared to St. Gertrude many times. He showed her his own Sacred Heart. Twice he let her rest her head on his Heart. Because of her great love for Jesus, her divine Spouse, Gertrude tried to correct her faults and become better. She trusted in him with her whole heart and was full of peace and joy.

St. Gertrude had a great devotion to Jesus in the Blessed Sacrament. She loved to receive Holy Communion often, even though in those days, it was not the custom. She was also very devoted to St. Joseph, the foster-father of Jesus. Sister Gertrude wrote many beautiful prayers. After suffering for about ten years, this saint went to join the Sacred Heart of Jesus, who made him her spouse.

We can grow in love for Jesus by being devoted to his Sacred Heart. St. Gertrude will help us understand and practice this devotion.

NOVEMBER 17

ST. ELIZABETH OF HUNGARY

This daughter of the king of Hungary was born in 1207. She married Louis, the ruler of Thuringia, while she was very young. (We celebrate the feast of Blessed Louis on September 11.) Elizabeth was a beautiful bride who dearly loved her handsome husband. Louis returned her affection with all his heart. God sent them three children and they were very happy for six years.

Then St. Elizabeth's sorrows began. Louis died of the plague. She was so heart-broken that she cried: "The world is dead to me and all that is joyous in the world." Louis' relatives had never liked Elizabeth because she had given so much food to the poor. While Louis was alive, they had not been able to do anything. Now, however, they could and they did. Within a short time, this beautiful, gentle princess and her three children were sent away from the castle. They suffered hunger and cold. Yet Elizabeth did not complain about her terrible sufferings. Instead she blessed God and prayed with great fervor. She accepted the sorrows just as she had accepted the joys.

Elizabeth's relatives came to her rescue. She and her children had a home once more. Her uncle wanted her to marry again, for she was still very young and attractive. But the saint had determined to give herself to God. She wanted to imitate the poverty of St. Francis. She went to live in a poor cottage and spent the last few years of her life serving the sick and the poor. She even went fishing to try to earn more money for her beloved poor. St. Elizabeth was only twenty-four when she died. On her death bed, she was heard to sing softly. She had great confidence that Jesus would take her to himself. Elizabeth passed away in 1231.

We can ask St. Elizabeth to teach us to take everything from the hands of God. If he sends us joys, we thank him. If he asks us to suffer a little, we offer it up as an act of love.

ST. ROSE PHILIPPINE DUCHESNE

This saint labored for Jesus in the United States. She was born into a wealthy French family in 1769. As a youngster, there was nothing especially holy about Rose. In fact, she often did her best to get her own way. She ordered everyone else to do what she wanted. In school, her favorite subject was history. She later became very interested in stories about Native Americans. At the age of seventeen, Rose entered the convent. She was not allowed to take her vows when the time came, because of the French Revolution. All the professed sisters were forced by the revolutionaries to leave the country, and Rose had to return to her family. Still she did not give up her desire to belong to Jesus. Several years later she joined the newly formed Religious of the Sacred Heart of Jesus.

Mother Rose Philippine Duchesne's great desire was to be a missionary. However, she was fifty before she was sent to the United States. It was still a mission land at this time. In Mississippi, she and a small group of sisters started a free school for the children of poor families. The work was hard, because of the different languages and ways of the people. Despite the many difficulties, Mother Duchesne never lost her youthful enthusiasm. As she grew older, she became less commanding and more gentle.

Mother Duchesne was a real heroine who went through terrible journeys. She nearly died from yellow fever. She overcame all kinds of obstacles to open convents in the New World. Then, when she was seventy-one, she resigned her position as superior. She went off to open a school among her beloved native people. She died in 1852 at the age of eighty-three and was proclaimed a saint by Pope John Paul II in 1988.

Sometimes we can have a way of postponing hard duties. We can ask Mother Duchesne to give us some of her stamina. She will help us put energy and love of God into what we do.

NOVEMBER 19

ST. NERSES

Nerses lived in fourth-century Armenia. He was an official in the court of King Arshak. After Nerses' wife died, he was ordained a priest. He became chief bishop of Armenia in 363. He and St. Basil worked to help the people become more fervent Catholics. They called a meeting of all the Armenian bishops. They wanted to help the priests and people grow in holiness.

Bishop Nerses appreciated the vocation of monks. He wanted new monasteries to begin. He started hospitals and encouraged the rich to be honest and generous. King Arshak was not living a good life. When he murdered his wife, Olympia, Bishop Nerses publicly condemned this terrible crime. The king banished Bishop Nerses from his diocese and appointed another bishop.

King Arshak was killed in battle against the Persians. His son became king. Unfortunately, the son did more evil than his father. Bishop Nerses corrected him. The new king pretended to be sorry. He invited the bishop to his palace for supper to show his good will. But the food was poisoned and Nerses died right there at the king's table. He is considered a martyr and the Armenians call him "the great."

Sometimes what we are asked to do is hard. It might seem to call for more courage than we have. At moments like that, we can call on St. Nerses and ask him to give us some of his courage.

NOVEMBER 20

ST. EDMUND

Edmund was an English king who lived in the ninth century. He became king when he was only fourteen. Yet his high position did not make him proud or conceited. Instead, he took as his model the Old Testament king, David. Edmund tried to serve God as well as David had. In fact, Edmund even learned David's psalms by heart. The psalms are beautiful hymns of praise to God contained in the Holy Bible.

King Edmund governed wisely, showing kindness to all his subjects. When Danish barbarians invaded his land, he fought them bravely. Their army was much larger than his. At last, the English king was captured. The barbarian leader offered to spare Edmund's life if he would agree to certain terms. But since these terms were opposed to his country and his religion, the king refused. He declared he would never save his life by offending God and his people. In anger, the pagan chief condemned him to death.

St. Edmund was tied to a tree and then cruelly whipped. The holy king took it all patiently, calling on Jesus for strength. Next, his torturers shot arrows into every part of his body. They were careful not to hit any vital organ, so his sufferings would be prolonged. At last he was beheaded. King Edmund died in 870.

Devotion to St. Edmund the martyr became very popular in England. Many churches were dedicated in his honor.

We can pray to St. Edmund for the loyalty to God and our country that he had.

PRESENTATION OF MARY

When she was only three years old, the Blessed Virgin Mary was taken to the Temple in Jerusalem by her parents, St. Joachim and St. Anne. (We celebrate their feast day on July 26.) Mary's whole life was to belong to God. He had chosen her to be the Mother of his Son, Jesus. The Blessed Virgin was happy to begin serving God in the Temple. And St. Joachim and St. Anne were pleased to offer their saintly little girl to God. They knew that God had sent her to them.

In the Temple, the high priest received the child Mary. She was placed among the girls who were dedicated to prayer and Temple service. The high priest kissed and blessed the holy child. He realized that the Lord had great plans for her. Mary did not weep or turn back to her parents. She came so happily to the altar that everyone in the Temple loved her at once.

St. Joachim and St. Anne went back home. They praised God for their blessed daughter. And Mary remained in the Temple, where she grew in holiness. She spent her days reading the Bible, praying and serving the Temple priests. She made beautiful linens and splendid vestments. Mary was loved by all the other girls because she was so kind. Mary tried to do each of her duties well, to please God. She grew in grace and gave great glory to the Lord.

Mary lived her life to please God. She was aware of his divine presence. We can ask Our Heavenly Mother Mary to teach us how to please Jesus every day.

ST. CECILIA

This patroness of music lived in early times. What we know about her goes back to the fourth century. Cecilia was a Roman noblewoman who had given her heart to Christ. Beneath the rich clothes worn by women of her class, Cecilia wore a rough shirt that caused her suffering. She wanted to be able to offer this sacrifice to Jesus, whose bride she intended to be. But Cecilia's father gave her in marriage to a young pagan noble. It is said that during the wedding celebration, the lovely bride sat apart. She was singing to God in her heart and praying for his help. When she and Valerian, her husband, were alone, she gathered up courage and said to him: "I have a secret to tell you. You must know that I have an angel of God watching over me. If you let me keep my promise to be Christ's bride only, my angel will love you as he loves me."

Valerian was surprised and said kindly, "Show me this angel. If he comes from God, I will do as you wish."

Cecilia said, "If you believe in the one true God

and receive the waters of Baptism, then you will see my angel." Valerian went to Bishop Urban and was received with joy. After he had professed his belief in the Christian religion, he was baptized and returned to St. Cecilia. There by the saint's side, the young man saw the splendid angel.

Valerian's brother, Tiburtius, learned of the Christian faith from Cecilia. She spoke so beautifully of Jesus that before long, he too was baptized. Together the two brothers performed many works of charity. When they were arrested for being Christians, they went bravely to death rather than give up their new faith in Jesus. St. Cecilia lovingly buried their bodies, before she too was arrested. She converted the very officers who tried to make her sacrifice to false gods. When she was put into a fire, it did not harm her. At last, a man was sent to behead her. He struck her neck three times, but Cecilia did not die right away. She lay on the floor of her own home unable to move. Yet by holding out three fingers of one hand, and one of the other, she still professed her belief in the Blessed Trinity.

St. Cecilia reminds us of our guardian angel. We can ask Cecilia to help us be devoted to our angel as she was to hers.

The current Roman calendar lists a saint and a blessed on November 23. Their stories are briefly presented here one after the other.

ST. COLUMBAN

Columban, the most famous of the Irish missionary-monks, lived in the seventh century. He had a good education as a boy. When he was a teenager, he decided to become a monk. His mother could not bear the thought of him leaving her. However, Columban felt the call to serve God in the quiet of a monastery. After many years as a monk in Ireland, Columban and twelve other monks set sail for France. There was a shortage of priests there at that time. The French people were inspired by the lives of the monks. These holy men performed penance, practiced devotion and lived in charity. Many young men were attracted to this holy way of life. They came and asked to join the monks. Soon the monks were building other monasteries to house all the disciples of St. Columban.

There were some people, however, who thought the rules of these monks were too strict. St. Columban also faced danger when he confronted the king about his sins. As a result, he and his Irish monks had to leave France. St. Columban, though fairly old, still tried to preach to unbelievers in Switzerland. When he was seventy, he went into Italy and defended the faith against the Arian heretics. In his letters to Pope St. Boniface IV, St. Columban proclaims his great devotion to the Holy Father. "All we Irish, living in the most distant parts of the earth," he says, "are bound to the Chair of St. Peter." He calls the pope the "leader of leaders."

In his last years, St. Columban built the great monastery of Bobbio in Italy. He died there on November 23, 615. After his death, both the Irish and the Italians were very devoted to this wonderful missionary.

St. Columban and his monks were very dedicated to their call. People loved and admired them. When we want to increase our own Christian dedication, we can pray to St. Columban.

BLESSED MIGUEL AUGUSTIN PRO

Miguel Pro was born in Guadalupe, Mexico, in 1891. He was destined to become a martyr of the twentieth century. The Mexican government's persecution of the Church began in 1910. Miguel joined the Jesuit novitiate in 1911. He was twenty years old, generous, courageous and lively. By 1914 the revolution had become severe. Jesuit novices were slipped out of the country. They were sent to foreign seminaries for their training. Miguel completed his priestly studies in Belgium and was ordained in 1926.

The young priest's health was poor. He was especially troubled with constant stomach pains. His return to Mexico was a joy on the one hand and suffering on the other. He saw his people suppressed by the government that should have been serving them. Father Pro realized that he could bring them spiritual comfort. He could forgive their sins through the sacrament of Reconciliation. He could bring them the Eucharistic Jesus to be their strength. And that he did. Miguel was ingenious at disguising himself. He slipped in and out of buildings and rooms and lives. He was always just on the verge of getting caught. Then he would slip out of sight.

Miguel Augustin Pro

Blessed

IHS

Father Pro performed his ministry heroically until November 23, 1927. He was caught and condemned for being a Catholic priest. He faced the firing squad and stretched out his arms until his whole body was like a living cross. Then he called in a loud clear voice: "Viva Cristo Rey!" (Long live Christ the King.)

President Calles forbade a public funeral. He threatened punishment for anyone who might attend. Yet people lined up along the streets where the body of the slain priest passed. They stood and prayed in their hearts, thanking God for the life and witness of Miguel Pro. He was proclaimed "blessed" by Pope John Paul II on September 25, 1988.

Blessed Miguel Pro lived at a time when Catholics were persecuted in Mexico. But he chose to follow his religious vocation just the same. We can ask Blessed Miguel Pro to give us the grace to love our Catholic faith as much as he did.

ST. ANDREW DUNG-LAC AND COMPANIONS

Christian missionaries first brought the Catholic faith to Vietnam during the sixteenth century. During the seventeenth, eighteenth and nineteenth centuries, Christians suffered for their beliefs. Many were martyred, especially during the reign of Emperor Minh-Mang (1820-1840). One hundred seventeen martyrs are in the group. They were proclaimed saints by Pope John Paul II on June 19,1988.

The group was made up of ninety-six Vietnamese, eleven Spaniards, and ten French. Eight of the group were bishops, fifty were priests and fifty-nine were lay Catholics. Some of the priests were Dominicans. Others were diocesan priests who belonged to the Paris Mission Society. One such diocesan priest was St. Theophane Venard. (We honor him also on November 6.) St. Andrew Dung-Lac, who represents this group of heroes, was a Vietnamese diocesan priest.

The martyrs of Vietnam suffered to bring the greatest treasure that they possessed: their Catholic faith.

We can join our prayers to the prayers of these martyrs for the Catholic Church in Vietnam. We can ask the Lord to bless this land that has suffered so much for centuries.

ST. CATHERINE OF ALEXANDRIA

Catherine lived in early Christian times. She was the daughter of a wealthy pagan couple of Alexandria, Egypt. She was a very beautiful girl whose great interest was in learning. Catherine loved to study deep questions of philosophy and religion. One day she began to read about Christianity. Soon she became a Christian.

St. Catherine was only eighteen when Emperor Maxentius began persecuting the Christians. Fearlessly, the lovely young Christian woman went to tell him what she thought of his cruelty. When he spoke of the pagan gods, she very plainly showed him that they were false. Maxentius could not answer her arguments. Therefore, he sent for fifty of his best pagan philosophers. Once again, it was Catherine who proved the truth of her religion. All fifty philosophers were convinced that she was right. In great fury, Maxentius had every one of them killed. Next, he tried to win her by offering her a queen's crown. When Catherine absolutely refused it, he had her beaten and thrown into prison.

While Maxentius was away at camp, his wife and an officer were very curious to hear this amazing Christian girl speak. They went to her cell. The result was that they and two hundred soldiers of the guard were converted. For this, they were all put to death. Catherine herself was placed on a wheel full of spikes to be tortured to death. When the wheel began to spin, it mysteriously snapped in two and fell apart. Finally, St. Catherine was beheaded. She has always been the patroness of Christian philosophers.

St. Catherine of Alexandria saw the beauty in her Christian beliefs. That is why she could so effectively convince others. We can ask St. Catherine to help us grow in love for the truths of our faith as she did.

NOVEMBER 26

ST. JOHN BERCHMANS

This Belgian saint once said, "If I do not become a saint when I am young, I shall never become one." In fact, he died at the early age of twenty-two—and he had, without any doubt, reached his goal of sanctity.

John was born in 1599. As a child, he stayed very close to his sick mother. Still, he liked to join with his young friends in putting on plays about Bible stories. He was especially good at playing the part of Daniel defending the innocent Susanna. By the time he was thirteen, he wanted to begin studying for the priesthood. However, his father, a shoemaker, needed his help in supporting the family. Finally, Mr. Berchmans decided to let John become a servant in the household of a priest. From there he could go to classes in the seminary.

Three years later, John Berchmans entered the Society of Jesus. He prayed, studied hard, and enthusiastically acted out parts in religious plays. He made a motto: "Have great care for little things," and he lived up to it. St. John Berchmans never performed any great, heroic deeds. But he did every little thing well, from waiting on tables to copying down notes on his studies.

When he became sick, no doctor could discover what illness he had. Yet John knew he was going to die. He was very cheerful as always. When the doctor ordered that his forehead be bathed with wine, John joked: "It's lucky that such an expensive sickness is not going to last long."

John Berchmans died in 1621. Miracles took place at his funeral. Right away people began to call him a saint.

This saint can be a model for every young person. He was a good son, a diligent student, and a dedicated Christian. John worked hard to become a saint. He prayed, especially to the Blessed Mother.

ST. JAMES INTERCISUS

James was a Persian who lived in the fifth century. He was a great favorite of King Yezdigerd I. When this king began to persecute Christians, James did not have the courage to confess his faith. He was afraid of losing the king's friendship. So he gave up his faith or at least pretended to. James' wife and mother were broken-hearted. When the king died, they wrote a strong letter to him to change his ways. This letter had its effect on James. He had been a coward, but at heart, he was still good. Now he began to stay away from court. He blamed himself openly for having given up his faith.

The new king sent for him, but this time, James hid nothing. "I am a Christian," he said. The king accused him of being ungrateful for all the honors his father, King Yezdigerd, had given him. "And where is your father now?" St. James calmly answered. The angry king threatened to put the saint to a terrible death. James replied, "May I die the death of the just."

The king and his council condemned James to torture and death. But his fears had gone. He said, "This death which appears so dreadful is very little for the purchase of eternal life." Then he told the executioners, "Begin your work." All the while, he kept declaring his faith that his body would one day rise in glory. St. James Intercisus died in 421.

When we make mistakes and our parents or teachers correct us, let us listen to them. They correct us because they love us. This saint made mistakes, but he listened to those who loved him.

NOVEMBER 28

ST. CATHERINE LABOURE

Zoe Laboure, born in 1806, was the daughter of a French farmer. She was the only one of her large family who did not go to school. She could not read or write. Her mother died while she was still very young. Zoe had to run the house when her older sister became a nun.

Zoe, too, would have liked to enter the convent when she was in her early teens. However, because she was needed at home, she waited until she was twenty-four. Zoe became a Sister of Charity of St. Vincent de Paul. She took the name of Catherine.

Shortly after she finished her training as a postulant, Sister Catherine received a special privilege. She began to see the Blessed Mother. One night, she was awakened from sleep. A "shining child" led her to chapel. There Our Lady came to talk to her. The Blessed Mother, in another vision, showed herself standing on a globe with streams of light coming from her hands. Underneath were the words: "O Mary, conceived without sin, pray for us who turn to thee!" Sister Catherine was told that a medal was to be made of this picture of Our Lady. She was also told that all who wore it would receive many graces from Jesus through his mother's prayers.

Sister Catherine told her confessor and he later told the bishop. So it was that the medal which we call the miraculous medal was made. Soon many, many people all over the world were wearing it. Yet no one in the convent knew that humble Sister Catherine was the one to whom Our Lady had appeared. She spent the remaining forty-five years of her life doing ordinary convent tasks. She answered the door. She looked after the hens that provided the nuns with eggs. She also took care of elderly and sick people. She was happy to keep her special privilege hidden, and was only interested in serving God as best she could. Catherine died in 1876. She was proclaimed a saint by Pope Pius XII in 1947.

We can wear the miraculous medal and often repeat the prayer: "O Mary, conceived without sin, pray for us who turn to thee."

BLESSED FRANCIS ANTHONY OF LUCERA

This saint, born in 1681, was nicknamed Johnny as a child. He was the son of an Italian farmer. His father died before he was ten. His mother's second husband was good to him. He sent the boy to be educated by the Franciscans.

When he was fifteen, Johnny asked to be admitted to the order. He became Brother Francis Anthony. He did very well in all his studies and became a priest. Father Francis Anthony became famous as a preacher and teacher. He also was elected superior. He tried his best to be of loving service to all the friars.

Father Francis Anthony had a special interest in prisoners. The prisons of his day were terrible places. He did his best to help the poor prisoners in every way. His love went out to everyone in need. It was he who began the custom of collecting gifts at Christmas time for poor families. In Lucera, the city in which he spent his life, it was said: "If you want to see St. Francis of Assisi, just look at Father Francis Anthony!"

Blessed Francis Anthony had a great devotion to Mary. He loved to pay special honor to her Immaculate Conception. It was at the beginning of the solemn novena for this feast that he died. Some time before, when he was in good health, he had said he would die soon. He had even suggested to a priest-friend that he come along. This good priest replied a bit excitedly, "Listen, Father, if you want to die, that is your affair, but I'm in no hurry!" What did the saint reply? "We must both make this journey," he said, "I first and you afterward." And that is just what happened. The other priest lived only two months after Blessed Francis Anthony passed to his eternal reward. Father Francis Anthony died in 1742 and was proclaimed "blessed" by Pope Pius XII in 1951.

The saints were not afraid to die because they often thought of heaven. We can ask Blessed Francis Anthony to show us today how to do everything for heaven.

ST. ANDREW

Andrew, like his brother, Simon Peter, was a fisherman. He became a disciple of the great St. John the Baptist. However, when John pointed to Jesus and said, "Behold the Lamb of God," Andrew understood that Jesus was greater. At once he left John to follow the Divine Master. Jesus knew that Andrew was walking behind him. Turning back, he asked, "What do you seek?" Andrew answered that he would like to know where Jesus dwelt. Our Lord replied, "Come and see." Andrew had been with Jesus only a little while when he realized that this was truly the Messiah. From then on, he decided to follow Jesus. He became the first disciple of Christ.

Next Andrew brought his brother Simon (St. Peter) to Jesus. The Lord received him, too, as his disciple. At first the two brothers continued to carry on their fishing trade and family affairs. Later, the Lord called them to stay with him all the time. He promised to make them fishers of men, and this time they left their nets for good. It is believed that after Our Lord ascended into heaven, St. Andrew preached the Gospel in Greece. He is said to have been put to death on a cross, to which he was tied, not nailed. He lived two days in that state of suffering. Andrew still found enough strength to preach to the people who gathered around their beloved apostle.

Two countries have chosen St. Andrew as their patron—Russia and Scotland.

When St. Andrew saw the cross on which he was to die, he exclaimed: "O good cross, made beautiful by Christ's body, you are welcome!" We can ask St. Andrew to help us recognize our particular cross. He will strengthen us to accept that cross generously.

ᕍecember

DECEMBER 1
ST. EDMUND CAMPION

Edmund lived in the sixteenth century. He was a very popular young English student who was a great speaker. In fact, Edmund was chosen to deliver a welcoming speech to Queen Elizabeth when she visited his college. A group of his fellow students were attracted by his happy nature and his many talents. They made him their leader. Even the queen and her chief ministers were fond of this attractive young man.

But Edmund was troubled about his religion. He kept thinking that the Catholic Church might be the only true Church. He did not hide his feelings. Therefore, the government, which was persecuting Catholics, became very suspicious of him. Edmund knew that he would lose the queen's favor and all his chances for a great career if he chose to become a Catholic. The young man prayed and reached his decision. He would become a Catholic anyway.

After he had escaped from England, Edmund studied to become a priest. He entered the Society of Jesus. When the Holy Father decided to send some Jesuits to England, Father Campion was one of the first to go. The night before he left, one of his fellow priests felt urged to write over his doorway: "Father Edmund Campion, martyr." Although he knew what danger faced him, the holy priest set out cheerfully. In fact, he had many a laugh because of his disguise as a jewel merchant. In England he preached with great success to Catholics who had to meet with him in secret. Spies of the queen's men were everywhere trying to catch him. He wrote: "I won't escape their hands much longer. Sometimes I read letters that say 'Campion has been caught'!" It was a traitor who finally brought about the Jesuit's capture. Edmund was visited in jail by the government officials who had been so fond of him. It seems that even Queen Elizabeth came. But none of their threats or promises could make him give up the Catholic faith. Nor could tortures break him. In spite of all his sufferings, he still defended himself and his fellow priests in such a marvelous manner that no one could answer him. Yet the enemies of the Church condemned him anyway. Before he was put to death, St. Edmund forgave the man who had betrayed him. He even helped save the man's life. St. Edmund Campion died in 1581. He was about forty-one years old.

We can pray to St. Edmund Campion for wisdom to acquire the Christian values he had.

DECEMBER 2

ST. BIBIANA

Bibiana's father Flavian had been prefect of the city of Rome in early Christian times. He and his wife were known as fervent Christians. In fact, when Emperor Julian left the Catholic faith, he began persecuting it. That is when Flavian was arrested. He was branded on the face with a hot iron and then exiled.

After he died, his wife Dafrosa was also made a prisoner in her own house. This was only because of her good Christian life. Then she, too, was put to death. Left alone with her sister, Demetria, Bibiana tried with all her heart to trust in God and pray. Everything they had was being taken from them. Then the two young women were brought to court. Poor Demetria was so frightened that she dropped dead at the judge's feet. Bibiana was handed over to a sinful woman, who was supposed to make the girl as evil as she was. This woman tried by sweet words and many clever tricks to make Bibiana fall. However, the saint could not be moved. She was brought back to court and beaten. Yet she held to her faith and purity as strongly as ever.

St. Bibiana was beaten to death with leaden scourges. A priest buried her at night beside her mother and sister.

Saint Francis Xavier

Sometimes we cannot understand why good people are allowed to suffer. It may seem also that people who do so much evil get away with it. When we feel confused about this, or resentful, we can ask St. Bibiana for help. She will show us how to judge from a Christian point of view.

DECEMBER 3

ST. FRANCIS XAVIER

This great missionary was born at Xavier Castle in Spain in 1506. He went to the University of Paris when he was eighteen. Here he met St. Ignatius Loyola, who was about to start the Society of Jesus. St. Ignatius tried to get Francis to join him. At first the happy-go-lucky young man would not think of it. St. Ignatius repeated to him the words of Jesus in the Gospel: "What does it profit a person to gain the whole world and lose his own soul?" At last, Francis saw clearly that his place in life was among the Jesuits.

When Francis was thirty-four, St. Ignatius sent him as a missionary to the East Indies. The king of Portugal wanted to give him presents to take along and a servant. Francis refused his kind offer and explained: "The best way to acquire true dignity is to wash one's own clothes and boil one's own pot." During the course of his amazing career in Goa, India, Japan and other lands of the east, St.

Francis made thousands of converts. In fact, he baptized so many people that he became too weak to raise his arms. He gathered the little children around him and taught them the Catholic faith. Then he made little lay apostles of them. He invited them to spread the faith they had learned. There was nothing St. Francis wouldn't do to help people. Once he faced a fierce band of raiders, alone, with no weapon but his crucifix. They backed up and did not attack his Christian tribes. The saint also brought many bad-living Christians to repentance. His only "tools" were his gentle, polite ways and his prayers.

In the midst of his painful journeys and great labors, the saint was full of a special joy coming from God. St. Francis longed to get into China, into which no foreigner was permitted. At last, the arrangements were made, but the great missionary became ill. He died almost alone in 1552 on an island off the Chinese coast. He was just forty-six-years-old. Francis Xavier was proclaimed a saint by Pope Gregory XV in 1622. He was in the best of company at the canonization ceremony in Rome. Ignatius of Loyola, Teresa of Avila, Philip Neri and Isidore the Farmer were also proclaimed saints that day.

We can ask St. Francis Xavier to give us understanding of and love for the missions. So many people still wait for the Gospel message. But they need generous missionaries to bring that message. We can pray to St. Francis Xavier and ask him to send many more holy missionaries to those who still wait.

DECEMBER 4

ST. JOHN DAMASCENE

St. John lived in the eighth century. He was born in the city of Damascus of a good Christian family. When his father died, he became the governor of Damascus. At this time, the emperor made a law. It forbade Christians from having statues or pictures of Our Lord and the saints. St. John Damascene knew the emperor was wrong. He joined with many others to defend this practice of the Christians. The pope himself asked John to keep telling people that it is a good thing to have statues and holy pictures. They make us think of Our Lord, the Blessed Mother and the saints. But the emperor would not give in to the Holy Father. He continued to forbid statues to be put in public places. St. John bravely wrote three letters. He told the emperor to give up his wrong ideas.

The emperor became so furious that he wanted revenge. John decided he should resign as governor. He gave away all his money to the poor and became a monk. He kept on writing marvelous books to defend the Catholic religion. At the same time he did all kinds of humble work in the monastery. One day he even went to sell baskets in the streets of Damascus. Many of those who had known him before were mean enough to laugh at him. Here was the man who had once been the great governor of the city now selling baskets.

Imagine how St. John must have suffered. But he knew that the money received would be put to good use at the monastery. He thought of Jesus, the Son of God, who wanted to be born in a stable. Then he felt happy to imitate Our Lord's humility.

St. John died a peaceful, happy death in the year 749.

The crucifix on our wall, the statues and pictures of saints remind us that our everlasting home is heaven. We can ask St. John Damascene to help us live in such a way that the Lord will welcome us into his eternal home someday.

DECEMBER 5

ST. SABAS

Sabas, born in 439, is one of the most famous monks of Palestine. His father was an officer in the army. When the officer had to go to Alexandria, Egypt, he left his young son with his brother-in-law. Since his aunt treated him badly, young Sabas ran away to another uncle. When an argument arose between the two uncles, Sabas felt terrible. He liked to see people at peace. So he ran away to live in a monastery. His two uncles felt ashamed of themselves. They told Sabas to come out and they would give him all his property. But by this time, Sabas was too happy in the monastery. He did not want to leave. Even though he was the youngest monk, he was the most fervent.

When he was eighteen, Sabas went to Jerusalem. He wanted to learn to live alone with God. He was advised to live in another monastery there for a while because he was still young. He obeyed and joyfully did all the hard work. He chopped wood for the fires and carried the heavy jugs of water. One day, St. Sabas was sent to Alexandria, Egypt, as the traveling companion of another monk. There he saw his father and mother! They tried their best to make him come with them. They wanted him to enjoy the same honors his father had won. Not Sabas! He would not even take the money they tried to give him. Finally he accepted three gold pieces. Then when he got back to the monastery, he gave them to the abbot.

At last, he was able to spend four years completely alone, as he desired. But after that, he had to start a new monastery. Many disciples came to him to learn how to be monks. Before long, he was put in charge of all the monks in Palestine.

Sometimes Sabas was sent to the emperor on important Church affairs. Even then, he wore his poor cloth habit, and kept to his hours of prayer. St. Sabas died in 532.

St. Sabas was a very prayerful person. He went out of his way to keep in touch with God. If we feel all noisy inside, we can say a prayer to St. Sabas. He will help us be peaceful and calm so that we can hear God's voice.

DECEMBER 6

ST. NICHOLAS

Nicholas is the great patron of children and of Christmas giving. He lived in the fourth century. Santa Claus is a short form of St. Nicholas. This famous saint was born in Asia Minor, which is modern-day Turkey. After his parents died, he gave all his money to charity.

Once a certain poor man was about to abandon his daughters to a life of sin because they did not have the money for a dowry. Nicholas heard about his problem. He went to the man's house at night and tossed a little pouch of gold through a window. This was for the oldest daughter. He did the same thing for the second daughter. The grateful father kept watch to find out who was being so good to them. When St. Nicholas came a third time, the man recognized him. He thanked Nicholas over and over again.

Later St. Nicholas became bishop. He loved justice. It is said that once he saved three men who had been falsely condemned to death. He then turned to their accuser. He made the man admit that he had been offered money to get rid of the three men.

St. Nicholas died in Myra, and a great basilica was built over his tomb. Many churches were dedicated in his name. When his relics were brought to Bari, Italy, this city became a famous shrine for pilgrims from all over Europe. Nicholas is the patron of sailors and prisoners. With St. Andrew, he is the patron of Russia.

We can learn from St. Nicholas how to have generous, loving hearts. He went out of his way to be good and do good to people. He will teach us how to be the same kind of person if we ask him.

DECEMBER 7

ST. AMBROSE

Ambrose was born around 340. He was the son of the Roman governor of Gaul. When his father died, his mother took her family back to Rome. She and her daughter, St. Marcellina, brought Ambrose up well. He became an outstanding lawyer. Then he was made governor of Milan and the territory around it. But by a strange event, Ambrose the governor became Ambrose the bishop. In those days the people used to suggest to the pope the name of the one they would like as bishop. To Ambrose's great surprise, the people of Milan chose him. He tried to escape, but it seemed to be God's will. Thus, Ambrose became a priest and then bishop of Milan.

Ambrose became a great model and father to his people. He also resisted all evil with amazing courage. He faced an attacking army and convinced the leader to turn back. Another time, Emperor Theodosius came from the east. He wanted to save Italy from invaders. He urged all his officers to respect the bishop of Milan. Yet when this emperor committed a very serious sin, Ambrose did not hesitate to confront him. He also made Theodosius do public penance. The emperor did not become furious and take revenge. He realized that the saint was right. Very humbly he publicly made penance for his sin. Ambrose had shown the world that no human being, even if he or she is the ruler, is higher than the Church.

People were afraid of what would happen to Italy when Ambrose died. When he became sick, they begged him to pray for a longer life. The saint replied, "I have not behaved myself among you in such a way that I should be ashamed to live longer; nor am I afraid to die, for we have a good Master."

Bishop Ambrose died on Good Friday in the year 397.

St. Ambrose became a great priest and bishop. He put his whole heart and energy into his ministry for God's people. We can ask him to help us value the priesthood. He will remind us to pray for priests.

DECEMBER 8

IMMACULATE CONCEPTION OF MARY

Our first parents offended God by sinning seriously. Because of the fall of Adam and Eve, every baby is born into the world with original sin. We are all children of our first parents. Therefore, we all inherit their sin. This sin in us is called original sin.

But the Blessed Virgin Mary was given a marvelous privilege. She was conceived in the womb of her mother, St. Anne, without this original sin. Our Lady was to be the mother of Jesus, God's only Son. The evil one, the devil, should have no power over Mary. There was never the slightest sin in our all-beautiful mother. That is why one of the Church's favorite hymns to Mary is: "You are all-beautiful, O Mary, and there is no sin in you."

This great privilege of Our Lady is called her Immaculate Conception. In 1854, Pope Pius IX proclaimed to the whole world that there was no doubt at all that Mary was conceived without sin. Four years later, she appeared to Bernadette at Lourdes. When St. Bernadette asked the lovely lady who she was, Mary joined her hands and raised her eyes toward heaven. She said, "I am the Immaculate Conception."

We can honor Mary as the Immaculate Conception with the prayer: "O Mary, conceived without sin, pray for us." We can also praise her by reciting three Hail Marys every morning and night.

BLESSED JUAN DIEGO

Juan Diego is well-known because the Mother of God appeared to him. It was to Juan Diego that Mary first introduced herself to the world as Our Lady of Guadalupe. He lived in the sixteenth century when Mexico City was known as the Valley of Anahuac. Juan was a member of the Chichimeca people. They called him the talking eagle. His Christian name was Juan Diego.

After Juan's particular mission was completed, it is said that he became a hermit. He spent the rest of his life in prayer and penance. His little hut was near the first chapel that was built on Tepeyac Hill. He was greatly esteemed. Parents considered it their fondest wish to have their children grow up to be like Juan Diego.

Juan took care of the little church and met the pilgrims who began to come there to honor their Mother of Guadalupe. He would show them the miraculous *tilma* or cloak that preserves Mary's beautiful image.

Pope John Paul II declared Juan Diego "blessed" on May 14, 1990. The pope personally visited the magnificent church of Our Lady of Guadalupe. He prayed there for all of the people of Mexico. He prayed especially for those who were killed during the terrible persecution of the Church in the early part of this century. He prayed for all the pilgrims who come to this beautiful church with such faith in the Mother of God.

Blessed Juan Diego was a prayerful, sensitive person. His lifestyle helped others see beyond the miraculous image of Guadalupe God's love for his people.

DECEMBER 10

ST. JOHN ROBERTS

John was born in Wales in 1577. Although he was not a Catholic, he was taught by an elderly priest. So, as he said later, at heart he was always a Catholic. John went to Oxford University in England for a while. Then he took a trip to France to have a good time. As it turned out, this trip brought him more than fun. It was in Paris, France, that he found great happiness in joining the Catholic Church. John lost no time after this in taking steps to become a priest. He went to an English college in Spain and became a Benedictine monk. Then his great dream of going back to England came true three years later. He and another monk were given permission to set out for that land. They knew the dangers they would meet. In fact, they did not have long to wait before trouble began. They entered England wearing plumed hats and swords at their sides. Soon, however, they were arrested for being priests and sent out of the country.

St. John Roberts went back to England again. He worked day and night to keep the faith alive during Queen Elizabeth's terrible persecution. Several times he was captured, put in prison, and exiled, yet he always came back. The last time Father John was arrested, he was finishing Mass. There was to be no escape. When asked, he declared he was a priest and a monk. He explained that he had come to England to work for the salvation of the people. "Were I to live longer," he added, "I would continue to do what I have been doing." St. John was given an unfair trial and condemned to death.

The night before he was to be hanged, a good Spanish lady arranged for him to be brought into the company of eighteen other prisoners. They were also suffering for Christ's sake. During their supper together, St. John was full of joy. Then he thought perhaps he should not show so much happiness. "Do you think I may be giving bad example by my joy?" he asked his hostess. "No, certainly not," she replied. "You could not do anything better than to let everyone see the cheerful courage you have as you are about to die for Christ."

The next day, St. John was hanged. The crowds were so attracted by the personality of this young priest that they did not let the executioners make him suffer. St. John Roberts was martyred in 1610.

Missionaries need our prayers because of the extra sacrifices they make. We can ask St. John Roberts to help us understand the important part that missionaries fulfill in Jesus' Church.

ST. DAMASUS I

Damasus was born in Rome and lived in the fourth century—exciting times for the Church. He was a priest who was generous and self-sacrificing. When Pope Liberius died in 366, Damasus became the pope. He faced many grave difficulties. There was a false pope named Felix. He and his followers persecuted Damasus. They lied about him, especially about his personal moral life. The pope had to stand trial before the Roman authorities. He was proved innocent, but he suffered very much through it all. His great friend, St. Jerome, spoke emphatically for the virtue of this pope. And Jerome had high standards. Pope Damasus realized that the city clergy were living too wealthy a lifestyle. The country priests were much more austere. Damasus asked the priests to simplify their lifestyles and not to accumulate money and possessions. He set a wonderful example himself.

There were also many false teachings during his time as pope. Damasus explained the true faith. He also called the Second Ecumenical Council which was held in Constantinople. Pope Damasus greatly encouraged love of the scriptures. He assigned St. Jerome to translate the Bible into Latin. He also changed the official language of the liturgy from Greek—except for the Kyrie—to Latin.

Pope St. Damasus died at the age of about eighty on December 11, 384. He was buried with his mother and sister in a little chapel he had built.

Pope St. Damasus shows us by his life that we can't let sufferings and troubles paralyze us. We have to do our tasks and live with enthusiasm no matter what people say about us. We can ask St. Damasus to show us the way to live responsibly every day.

DECEMBER 12

OUR LADY OF GUADALUPE

We celebrate the feast of Blessed Juan Diego on December 9. With just a few days in between, we celebrate the event of Mary's appearances on Tepeyac Hill in Mexico. The heavenly visitor came to her people on December 9, 1531. Juan was a fifty-five year old Catholic convert. He was going to Mass when Our Lady intercepted him as he was making his way down Tepeyac Hill. Mary asked him to go to the bishop. She wanted a great church built on the very spot where she was standing. The Indian was overwhelmed. He wanted with all his heart to do what the Lady commanded. But how could he approach the bishop? How could anyone believe such an unusual request? Juan Diego went to the bishop. The bishop must have been pleased with himself when he thought of a way to handle the situation. "Ask for a sign," he told Juan. Juan was caught in the middle. The Lady knew what she wanted; the bishop had the power to make her wish come true, but he wanted proof.

On the early morning of December 12, Juan Diego was hurrying along the path. His uncle was dying and he was going for the priest. Mary met Juan and told him that his uncle was better. In fact, Juan found out a little later that his uncle had been cured at that moment. The Lady asked Juan to go back to the bishop. She wanted him to build a church. Juan remembered the bishop's request and asked Mary for a sign. Mary sent Juan into the rocky area nearby and told him to gather the roses that were there. Juan was puzzled. He knew there were no roses. It was winter and the bushes were bare. But Juan followed the instructions and there really were roses, beautiful roses. Juan picked them all and went to the bishop. He carried them carefully in his *tilma* (cloak). Juan clutched his cloak and made his way into the room where the bishop was. Slowly he let down his cloak and the beautiful roses fell to the floor. Juan smiled and then realized that something else was capturing the bishop. He followed the bishop's eyes which were riveted to his cloak. And then he saw her, his beautiful lady, on his *tilma*. Her image was life-size, exactly as she had appeared. The bishop had received his sign and Mary would have her church.

Today a great church, called a basilica, marks the event when Our Lady of Guadalupe came to her people. Our Lady of Guadalupe was named patroness of Mexico by Pope Benedict XIV. She is also patroness of Latin America and the Philippines.

We can pray to Our Lady of Guadalupe for the graces we most need. She is a gentle and good mother who will speak to the Heart of her Son.

DECEMBER 13

ST. LUCY

This beloved saint lived in Syracuse, Sicily. She was born toward the end of the third century. Lucy was the daughter of very noble and rich parents. Her father died when she was still young. Lucy secretly promised Jesus that she would never marry so that she could be his alone. She was a lovely girl, with beautiful eyes. More than one young noble set his heart on her. Her mother urged her to marry one whom she had chosen for Lucy. But the girl would not consent. Then she thought of a plan to win her mother. She knew her mother was suffering from hemorrhages. She convinced her to go to the shrine of St. Agatha and pray for her recovery. Lucy went along with her and together they prayed. When God heard their prayers and cured her mother, Lucy told her of her vow to be Christ's bride. Her mother let Lucy follow her vocation, out of gratitude for her cure.

But the young pagan to whom she had promised Lucy was furious at losing out. In his bitter anger, he accused her of being a Christian. He threatened her with the frightening torture of being blinded. But Lucy was even willing to lose both her eyes rather than belong to anyone but Jesus. And that is just what happened. Many statues show St. Lucy holding her lovely eyes in the palm of her hand. Jesus rewarded her for her heroic love. He worked a miracle and gave her back her eyes, more beautiful than ever.

The pagan judge tried to send the saint to a house of sinful women. He hoped that Lucy might be tempted to give up Christ. But when they tried to carry her away, God made her body so heavy that they could not budge her. In the end, she was stabbed and became a martyr for Jesus in the year 304.

St. Lucy's beautiful eyes remind us of the wonderful faith that lit her soul. We can ask St. Lucy to help us grow in the kind of faith she had.

DECEMBER 14

ST. JOHN OF THE CROSS

John was born in Spain in 1542. He was the son of a weaver. He went to a school for poor children and became a servant to the director of a hospital. For seven years, John worked as a servant while also studying at a Jesuit college. Even as a youth, he liked to do penance. He understood the value of offering up sufferings for the love of Jesus. When he was twenty-one, his love of God prompted him to enter the Carmelite order. With St. Teresa of Avila, St. John was chosen by God to bring a new spirit of fervor among religious. But his life was full of trials. Although he succeeded in opening new monasteries where his holy way of life was practiced, he himself was criticized. He was even thrown into prison and made to suffer terribly. At one time, too, he had fierce temptations. God seemed to have left him alone, and he suffered greatly. Yet when these storms of trouble passed, the Lord rewarded his faithful servant. He gave him deep peace and joy of heart. John was very close to his God. In fact, the Blessed Mother herself showed John how to escape from his prison cell.

St. John had a marvelous way with sinners. Once a beautiful but sinful woman tried to make him do wrong. He talked to her so that she was led to change her life. Another lady, instead, had such a temper that she was nicknamed "the terrible." Yet St. John knew how to calm her down by his kind manners.

St. John of the Cross asked God to let him suffer every day for love of Jesus. To reward him, Our Lord revealed himself to St. John in a special way. This saint is famous for his spiritual books which show us how to grow close to God. He died on December 14, 1591. John of the Cross was proclaimed a Doctor of the Church by Pope Pius XI in 1926.

When we come up against something that is very hurtful or difficult, this is the saint to ask for help. He will let us see sufferings as opportunities to show our love for Jesus.

DECEMBER 15

ST. NINO

Nino was a Christian girl who lived in the fourth century. She was captured and carried off to Iberia as a slave. In that pagan country, her goodness and purity made a great impression on the people. Noticing how much she prayed, they asked her about her religion. The simple answer she gave them was that she adored Jesus Christ as God.

God chose this pure, devout slave-girl to bring Christianity to Iberia. One day, a mother brought her sick child to Nino, asking her to suggest a cure. The saint wrapped the baby in her cloak. Then she told the mother that Jesus Christ can cure the worst cases of sickness. She handed the child back and the mother saw that her child was completely cured. The queen of Iberia learned of this miracle. Since she herself was sick, she went to the saint. When she, too, was healed, she tried to thank the Christian girl. However, Nino said: "It is Christ's work, not mine. And he is the Son of God who made the world."

The queen let the king know the whole story of her cure. She repeated to her husband what the slave-girl had said of Jesus Christ. Shortly after this, the king got lost in a fog while out hunting. Then he remembered what his wife had told him. He said that if Jesus Christ would lead him safely home, he would believe in him. At once, the fog lifted, and the king was true to his promise.

St. Nino herself taught the king and queen the truths of Christianity. They gave her permission to teach the people. Meanwhile, the king began building a Christian church. Then he sent messengers to the Christian emperor, Constantine, to tell him of his conversion. He asked the emperor to send bishops and priests to Iberia.

So it was that a poor slave brought a whole country into the Church.

If we are humble, God will use us to do much good for his people. We can ask St. Nino to help us take advantage of the graces God offers us for becoming more humble.

DECEMBER 16

ST. ADELAIDE

St. Adelaide was born in 931. At the age of sixteen, this Burgundian princess was married to King Lothair. Three years later, her husband died. The ruler who is believed to have poisoned him tried to get Adelaide to be his wife. She absolutely refused. In anger, he treated her with great cruelty. He even locked her up in a castle on a lake.

Adelaide was saved when King Otto the Great of Germany conquered this ruler. Although she was twenty years younger than he, Otto married the lovely Adelaide on Christmas Day. When he took his new queen back home, the German people loved her at once. She was as gentle and gracious as she was pretty. God sent five children to the royal couple. They lived happily for twenty-two years. When Otto died, Adelaide's oldest son became the ruler. This son, Otto the Second, was good, but too quick to act without thinking. He turned against his own mother and she left the palace. In her great sorrow, she appealed to the abbot, St. Majolus. He made Otto feel sorry for what he had done. Adelaide met her son in Italy and the king begged her forgiveness. She in turn prayed for her son, sending offerings to the great shrine of St. Martin of Tours.

In her old age, St. Adelaide was called on to rule the country while her grandson was still a child. She started many monasteries and convents and worked to convert the Slavic people. All her life, this saintly empress had obeyed the advice of holy people. She had always been willing to forgive those who had hurt her. St. Addle of Cluny called her a "marvel of beauty and grace."

She died on December 16, 999.

St. Adelaide was beautiful not just because of her physical features. She was a beautiful person because she was deeply Christian and a woman who lived her Catholic values. We can ask her to show us how to be Christians true to our values as she was.

ST. OLYMPIAS

This saint was born around the year 361. She belonged to a great family of Constantinople. When she was left an orphan, she was given into the care of a wonderful Christian woman. Olympias had inherited a large fortune and was both sweet and attractive. So her uncle found it easy to marry her to Nebridius, a man who had been governor of Constantinople. St. Gregory Nazianzen apologized for not being able to attend the wedding. He even sent a poem full of good advice for Olympias.

Nebridius died very soon afterward, however, and the emperor urged Olympias to marry again. She answered: "Had God wished me to remain a wife, he would not have taken Nebridius away." And she refused to marry again. St. Gregory called her "the glory of the widows in the Eastern Church." With a number of other pious ladies, Olympias spent her life performing works of charity. She dressed plainly and prayed much. She gave her money away to everyone. Finally, St. John Chrysostom had to tell her to be careful in giving away her goods. "You must not encourage the laziness of those who live upon you without necessity," he said. "It is like throwing your money into the sea."

St. John Chrysostom became archbishop of

Constantinople. As their archbishop, he guided St. Olympias and her disciples in their works. The women started a home for orphans and they opened a chapel. They were able to give help to great numbers of people. St. John Chrysostom became Olympias' dearest guide. When he was exiled, she was deeply grieved. She then had to suffer persecution, too. Her community of widows and single women was forced to stop their charitable works. Besides this, Olympias was in poor health and was being criticized. Yet St. John wrote to her: "I cannot stop calling you blessed. The patience and dignity with which you have borne your sorrows, your prudence, wisdom and charity have won you great glory and reward."

St. Olympias died in 408, when she was about forty. Someone described her as "a wonderful woman, like a precious vase filled with the Holy Spirit."

St. Olympias received many blessings from God. She used those gifts—her time, money and talents—to help people. We can ask St. Olympias to show us our gifts and to help us use them for others.

DECEMBER 18

ST. FLANNAN

Flannan lived around the seventh century. He was the son of an Irish chieftain named Turlough. Flannan was educated by the monks. He also learned farming from them. When he was a grown man, Flannan decided to make a pilgrimage to Rome. In Rome, Pope John IV made him a bishop. The pope did this because he recognized the wisdom and holiness of the man. When St. Flannan returned to Ireland, all the people of his region, Killaloe, came to meet him. They were eager to learn the instructions the saint had brought back from the pope of Rome.

St. Flannan taught his people so well that even his father decided to become a monk. The old chieftain went to St. Colman to be instructed in the life of a monk. At the same time, he asked for a blessing for his family, since three of his sons had been killed. St. Colman predicted: "From you shall seven kings spring." And so it happened.

St. Flannan was afraid that since he was one of the family, he, too, might be made king. So he prayed to become ugly, and his face was soon covered with big scars and rashes. He made this unusual request because he wanted to be free to follow his vocation. He wanted to devote himself entirely to the service of God and his people.

St. Flannan decided to put God first in his life. That is why he could be so true to his calling. We all have a special place in God's plan. He offers us the opportunity to give our gifts for others in some way. But we have to make him first in our lives, so that we can hear his voice. We can ask St. Flannan to help us.

DECEMBER 19

BLESSED URBAN V

Blessed Urban's name before he became pope was William de Grimoard. He was born in France in 1310 and became a Benedictine monk. After being given many high positions, he became pope. At this time, the pope lived in a city called Avignon, in France. However, Urban made up his mind to go to Rome, because that is where the pope should live. The pope is the bishop of Rome, and Urban knew that his place was in Rome. There were many difficulties. The people in France objected to his going, but Urban did what he felt was right.

The people of Rome were overjoyed to have the pope back. They were especially joyful to have such a holy man as was Urban V. He set about at once to repair the great churches of Rome. He helped the poor, and encouraged the people to be fervent and devout again. Emperor Charles V showed great respect to the Holy Father. But Urban had a great many problems. For one thing, he was getting sicker and weaker all the time. Many of his cardinals kept urging him to go back to Avignon. So at last he gave in. As he prepared to leave Rome, the people of the city begged him to stay. He was very sad, but left anyway. About three months later, he died. It was in the year 1370.

It was not right for Urban to leave Rome, because as the bishop of Rome he belonged there. But aside from this weakness, he was a very holy and good man. He did much for the Church, for schools and universities, and for the people. He was called "a light of the world and a way of truth."

The pope has many and serious responsibilities. Let us remember to pray every day for our present pope. We can say: "Lord, cover with your protection our Holy Father, the pope. Be his light, his strength, his comfort."

DECEMBER 20

ST. DOMINIC OF SILOS

Dominic, a Spanish shepherd boy, was born at the beginning of the eleventh century. He spent many hours alone with his sheep at the bottom of the Pyrenees mountains. It was there that he learned to love to pray. Soon he became a monk and a very good one. Dominic was appointed abbot of his monastery and brought about many changes for the better.

One day, however, King Garcia III of Navarre, Spain, claimed that some of the monastery's possessions were his. St. Dominic refused to give them to the king. He did not think it was right to give the king what belonged to the Church. This decision greatly angered the king. He ordered Dominic to leave his kingdom. Abbot Dominic and his monks were given a friendly welcome by another king, Ferdinand I of Castile. Ferdinand told them they could have an old monastery called St. Sebastian at Silos. This monastery was located in a lonely spot and was very run-down. But with Dominic as the abbot, it soon began to take on a new look. In fact, he made it one of the best known monasteries in all Spain.

St. Dominic worked many miracles to cure all kinds of sicknesses.

Many years after his death, Dominic appeared to a wife and mother. Her name was Joan. Now she is called Blessed Joan of Aza. Dominic told her that God would send her another son. When that son was born, Joan gratefully named him Dominic. And this son became the great St. Dominic, founder of the Dominican order. We celebrate his feast on August 8. Today's saint died on December 20, 1073.

St. Dominic of Silos shows us by his life that prayer is as essential to us as breathing and eating. We can ask St. Dominic to remind us often each day of our need to talk to God.

ST. PETER CANISIUS

Peter, a Dutch man, was born in 1521. His father wanted him to be a lawyer. To please him, young Peter began to study law before he had finished all his other studies. Soon enough, however, he realized that he would never be happy in that life. About that time, people all over were talking about the wonderful preaching of Blessed Peter Faber. He was one of the first members of the Jesuit order. When Peter Canisius listened to him, he knew he, too, would be happy serving God as a Jesuit. So he joined the order. After more years of study and prayer, he was ordained a priest.

The great St. Ignatius soon realized what an obedient and zealous apostle St. Peter Canisius was. He sent him to Germany where Peter labored for forty years. It would be hard to name all St. Peter Canisius' great works, prayers and sacrifices during that time. His concern was to save many cities of Germany from the heresies of the day. He also labored to bring back to the Catholic Church those who had accepted false teachings. It is said that he traveled about twenty thousand miles in thirty years. This he did on foot or on horseback. In spite of all this, St. Peter Canisius still found time to write many books on the faith. He realized how important books are. So he made a campaign to stop bad books from being sold. And he did all he could to spread good books to teach the faith. The two catechisms St. Peter Canisius wrote were so popular that they were printed over two hundred times and were translated into fifteen languages.

To those who said he worked too hard, St. Peter Canisius would answer, "If you have too much to do, with God's help, you will find time to do it all." This wonderful saint died in 1597. He was proclaimed a Doctor of the Church by Pope Pius XI in 1925.

We want to learn about our faith with enthusiasm, the way St. Peter Canisius did. We can ask him to help us study hard and frequently.

ST. CHAEREMON, ST. ISCHYRION AND OTHER MARTYRS

The third century was marked by Roman persecutions of the Church. Today's saints were martyred during the reign of Emperor Decius. They lived in Egypt. Many of the Christians were driven out into the desert. There they died in a variety of ways: hunger, thirst, cold nights, wild animals, criminals. Naturally, if the Christians tried to return to civilization, they were killed. The young, healthy Christians were sold into slavery.

St. Chaeremon was a priest and bishop of Nilopolis. He was very old when the persecution became extreme. The elderly bishop and a companion went for shelter to the mountains of Arabia. They were never seen again, nor were their bodies ever found.

St. Ischyrion worked for an official in one of Egypt's cities. It may have been Alexandria. His employer required that he sacrifice to the gods. Ischyrion refused because this was against the first commandment. The official was angry and insulted. He had Ischyrion killed.

A great many other martyrs are included here who gave their lives for Jesus at this time in Egypt.

We can be angered at the way the Christian martyrs were treated. And this is understandable. But we also might have to admit that sometimes we are thoughtless and even mean with people. We can ask today's martyrs to teach us how to be loving and forgiving. They will also show us how to be kind and respectful with everyone.

The current calendar lists two saints on December 23.
Their stories are briefly presented here one after the other.

ST. JOHN OF KANTY

This Polish saint was born in 1390, the son of good country folk. Seeing how intelligent their son was, they sent him to the University of Krakow. He did well in his studies. Then John became a priest, a teacher, and a preacher. He was also well-known for his great love of the poor. Once he was eating in the university dining hall. At the beginning of the meal, he happened to see a beggar passing by the window. Immediately, he jumped up and brought the man his dinner.

Some people became very jealous of St. John's success as a teacher and preacher. They finally managed to have him sent to a parish as a pastor. Here, he put his whole heart into the new life. At first, however, things did not go well at all. The people did not particularly care for John, and John was afraid of the responsibility. He did not give up, however, and his efforts brought results. By the time he was called back to the university, the people of his parish loved him dearly. They went part of the way with him. In fact, they were so sad to see him go that he had to tell them: "This sadness does not please God. If I have done any good for you in all these years, sing a song of joy."

Back in Krakow, St. John taught Bible classes and again became a very popular teacher. He was invited to the homes of rich nobles. Still, however, he gave everything he had to the poor and dressed very poorly himself. Once he wore an old black habit, called a cassock, to a banquet. The servants refused to let him in. St. John went home and changed into a new one. During the dinner, someone spilled a dish of food on the new cassock. "Never mind," said the saint with good humor, "my cassock deserves some food, anyway, because without it, I wouldn't have been here at all."

St. John lived to be eighty-three. Again and again during all those years he cleaned out everything he owned to help the poor. When people burst into tears on hearing that he was dying, he said, "Don't worry about this prison which is decaying. Think of the soul that is going to leave it." He died in 1473 and was proclaimed a saint by Pope Clement XIII in 1767.

We can learn from St. John of Kanty to do our studying and our work with diligence. God expects us to do the best we can and he will bless our efforts. We can ask St. John of Kanty to help us do our best.

ST. MARGUERITE D'YOUVILLE

Marguerite was born in Quebec, Canada, on October 15, 1701. Her father died in 1708 and the family lived in poverty. Relatives paid her tuition at the Ursuline convent school in Quebec. Her two years at the boarding school prepared her to teach her younger brothers and sisters. Marguerite was gracious and friendly. She helped support her family by making and selling fine lace. In 1722, Marguerite married Francois D'Youville. It seemed like the marriage was going to be a truly happy one. But Francois' real self came out as the months passed. He was more interested in making money than in being with his family. His job was illegal liquor trading. He left Marguerite alone with her two children and did not take care of them.

Francois died quite suddenly in 1730 after eight years of marriage. He left Marguerite with large debts to pay. A kind priest named Father du Lescoat gave her courage. He told her that she was loved by God. Soon she would begin a great work for God. The prophecy would come true. Mother D'Youville took in a blind, homeless woman on November 21, 1737. This marks the beginning of a marvelous work of caring for the sick poor in hospitals. These hospitals would be run by the sisters of her new order. She and her first companions became known as the "Grey Nuns." Their religious habit was grey. The sisters took over the general hospital in Montreal. It was run-down and very much in debt. People made fun of the sisters. What were they trying to do, anyway? But Mother D'Youville and her sisters did not lose heart. They worked, and built, and fixed. Above all, they welcomed everyone in need. No one was too poor or too sick to come to their hospital. In 1765, a fire destroyed the hospital, but Mother D'Youville and her nuns had it rebuilt in four years.

Marguerite's two boys became priests: Charles, pastor of Boucherville, and Francois, pastor of St. Ours. In 1769, Father Francois broke his arm. His mother hastened to take care of him. She spent five days at the rectory. Mother D'Youville was equally generous when an epidemic of smallpox spread through the Indian missions of Montreal. And during the Seven Years War between the French and British, she helped soldiers on both sides. She hid the British soldiers in the dark rooms of the convent cellar. There her sisters quietly nursed them back to health.

Mother Marguerite D'Youville died on December 23, 1771. She was proclaimed a saint by Pope John Paul II on December 9, 1990. She is Canada's first Canadian-born saint.

Mother D'Youville's life was hard, but the Lord worked wonderfully through the difficulties. When things seem hard for us, we can ask St. Marguerite D'Youville to give us some of her courage and cheerfulness.

DECEMBER 24

ST. CHARBEL

St. Charbel was born Youssef Makhlouf on May 8, 1828, in a mountain village in Lebanon. His life was very ordinary. Youssef attended the small school and the parish church. He loved the Blessed Mother and he loved to pray. He had two uncles who were monks. Although Youssef did not tell anyone, he prayed to Our Lady to ask her help in becoming a monk. His parents wanted him to marry. There was a very nice girl in the village who would make an ideal wife, they thought. But Youssef believed it was time to follow his call to become a monk. He joined the monastery of Our Lady at the age of twenty-three. He took the name Charbel, after an early martyr by that name. He professed solemn vows in 1853 when he was twenty-five. Charbel studied for the priesthood and was ordained in 1858. He remained at the monastery of St. Maron for sixteen years.

Father Charbel was a profound person whose love for prayer became his outstanding quality. From time to time he would retreat to the order's hermitage for stronger prayer times. The last twenty-three years of his life, Charbel spent in the peace of the hermitage. He chose to lead a very hard life. He made sacrifices, ate little, slept on the hard ground, and prayed long hours. The years passed, and Charbel became a person totally in love with Jesus. Then as he celebrated the Mass on December 16, 1898, he suffered a stroke during the consecration. Charbel lingered for eight painful days, then died on December 24, 1898.

Miracles began to happen at the holy monk's grave. Some of those miracles were accepted for declaring Charbel "blessed" and then "saint." Father Charbel was proclaimed a saint by Pope Paul VI on October 9, 1977. The pope explained that St. Charbel taught us by his life the true way to God. He said that our culture glorifies wealth and comfort. Charbel, instead, teaches by his example the value of being poor, self-sacrificing and prayerful.

We can ask St. Charbel to share with us his love for prayer. We can also ask him to bless and protect all the suffering people of his homeland.

DECEMBER 25

CHRISTMAS
THE BIRTHDAY OF JESUS

The time had come for the Son of God to become man for love of us. His mother Mary and St. Joseph had to leave their home in Nazareth and go to Bethlehem. The reason for this journey was the Roman emperor's request to count the number of his subjects. So every Jewish family had to go to the city of their ancestors. Since Mary and Joseph belonged to the royal family of David, they had to go to David's city of Bethlehem. The emperor had made the law, but it served to fulfill God's plan. The Bible said that the Savior was to be born in Bethlehem.

It was a slow, hard journey for our Blessed Mother over mountainous country. But Mary was calm and peaceful. She knew she was doing God's will. She was happy thinking of her Divine Son soon to be born. When Mary and Joseph reached Bethlehem, they found that there was no place for them to stay. At last, they found shelter in a cave. There, in that rough stable, the Son of God was born on Christmas Day. His Blessed Mother wrapped him up warmly and laid him in a manger. Our Lord chose to be born in such poverty so that we would learn not to desire riches and comforts. The very night in which Jesus was born, God sent his angels to announce his birth. The angels were not sent to the emperor or the king. They were not sent even to the learned doctors and chief priests. They were sent to poor, humble shepherds. These men were watching their flocks on the hillside near Bethlehem. As soon as they heard the angels' message, they hurried to adore the Savior of the world. Then they went home giving praise and glory to God.

The great patriarchs and prophets of the Old Testament had been comforted by the thought that someday the Savior would come into the world. Now he had been born among us. Christ came for all of us. The Bible says: "God so loved the world that he sent his only-begotten Son." If those who

327

lived in the hope of his coming were happy, how much more ought we to rejoice. We have his teachings, his Church and Jesus himself on our altars at every Eucharistic Celebration. Christmas is the time when we realize more than ever how much God loves us.

We can say a prayer to Mary and Joseph. We can ask them to help us know the gift that Jesus most wants to receive from us on Christmas Day.

DECEMBER 26

ST. STEPHEN

Stephen's name means crown. He was the first disciple of Jesus to receive the martyr's crown. Stephen was a deacon in the early Church. We read about him in chapters 6 and 7 of the Acts of the Apostles. Peter and the apostles had found that they needed helpers to look after the care of widows and the poor. So they ordained seven deacons. Stephen is the most famous of these.

God worked many miracles through St. Stephen. He spoke with such wisdom and grace that many of his hearers became followers of Jesus. The enemies of the Church of Jesus were furious to see how successful St. Stephen's preaching was. At last, they laid a plot for him. They could not answer his wise arguments, so they got men to lie about him. These men said that he had spoken sinfully against God. St. Stephen faced that great assembly of enemies without any fear. In fact, the Holy Bible says that his face looked like the face of an angel.

Stephen spoke about Jesus, showing that he is the Savior God had promised to send. He scolded his enemies for not having believed in Jesus. At that, they rose up in great anger and shouted at him. But Stephen looked up to heaven. He said that he saw the heavens opening and Jesus standing at the right hand of God. His hearers plugged their ears and refused to listen to another word. They dragged St. Stephen outside the city of Jerusalem and stoned him to death. The saint prayed, "Lord Jesus, receive my spirit!" Then he fell to his knees and begged God not to punish his enemies for killing him. After such an expression of love, the martyr went to his heavenly reward.

St. Stephen had a forgiving heart. He did not let himself give in to thoughts or actions of revenge. We can ask him to obtain for us the grace to forgive and forget when someone has hurt us.

DECEMBER 27

ST. JOHN THE APOSTLE

St. John was a fisherman in Galilee. He was called to be an apostle with his brother, St. James. Jesus gave these sons of Zebedee the nickname, "sons of thunder." St. John was the youngest apostle. He was dearly loved by the Lord. At the Last Supper, it was John who was permitted to lean his head on the chest of Jesus. John was also the only apostle who stood at the foot of the cross. The dying Jesus gave the care of his Blessed Mother Mary to this beloved apostle. Turning to Mary, he said, "Behold your mother." So the rest of her life on earth, the Blessed Mother lived with St. John. He alone had the great privilege of honoring and assisting the all-pure Mother of God.

On Easter morning, Mary Magdalene and the other women went with spices to Jesus' tomb to anoint his body. They came running back to the apostles with exciting news. The body of Jesus was gone from the tomb. Peter and John set out to investigate. John arrived first but waited for Peter to go in ahead of him. Then he went in and saw the neatly folded linen cloths. Later that same week, the disciples were fishing on the lake of Tiberias without success. A man standing on the beach suggested they let down their nets on the other side of the boat. When they pulled it up again it was full of large fish. Now John, who knew who this man was, called to Peter, "It is the Lord." With the descent of the Holy Spirit the apostles were filled with new courage. After the Ascension, Peter and John cured a crippled man by calling on the name of Jesus.

John lived nearly a century. He himself was not martyred, but he did lead a life of suffering. He preached the Gospel, and became bishop of Ephesus. In the last years of his life, when he could no longer preach, his disciples would carry him to the crowds of Christians. His simple message was, "My dear children, love one another." St. John died in Ephesus around the year 100.

We can ask St. John to teach us how to be sensitive to the feelings of others. We can also ask him to help us `*practice charity in what we think and say.*

DECEMBER 28

THE HOLY INNOCENTS

When Jesus was born in Bethlehem, the Wise Men came from the east to worship him. Some say they were kings, others astrologers. They went to Herod, the king, seeking the newborn king of the Jews, the Savior. Herod was a cruel, clever tyrant. When he heard these Wise Men speak of a newborn king, he began to worry about losing his throne. But he did not let the Wise Men know what he was thinking. He called in his chief priests and asked them where the Bible says the Messiah was to be born. They answered: Bethlehem.

"Go and find out about this child," the wicked king said to the Wise Men. "When you have found out where he is, come and tell me. Then I, too, will go and worship him." The Wise Men went on their way. They found Jesus the Messiah, with Mary and Joseph. They adored him and offered their gifts. Meanwhile, they were warned in their sleep not to go back to Herod. And an angel came to tell St. Joseph to take Mary and Baby Jesus into Egypt. In this way, God spoiled the murderous plans of Herod concerning the Divine Child.

When Herod realized that the Wise Men had not come back to him, he became furious. He was an evil, violent man, and now the fear of losing his throne made him worse. He sent his soldiers to kill all the boy babies of Bethlehem in the hope of killing the Messiah, too. The soldiers carried out the bloody order. There was great sorrow in the little town of Bethlehem, as mothers wept over their murdered babies. These little children are honored today by the Church as martyrs. They are called the Holy Innocents.

We can ask the Holy Innocents to protect all children from harm. We can ask them to change the hearts of those who promote abortion. We can also pray for those who abuse and neglect children.

DECEMBER 29

ST. THOMAS BECKET

Thomas Becket was born in 1118, in London, England. After his parents died, he went to work in an office. As a young man, he loved hunting and other sports. When Thomas was about twenty-four, he found a position in the household of the archbishop of Canterbury. He began to study to become a priest. He was handsome, very intelligent and pleasant to talk with. Before long, he became a great favorite of King Henry II himself. People said that the king and Thomas had only one heart and one mind—such close friends were they. When Thomas was thirty-six, King Henry made him his chancellor.

As chancellor of England, Thomas had a large household and lived in splendor. Yet he was also very good to the poor. Although Thomas was proud and quick-tempered, he performed many hidden acts of penance. He prayed long hours, often into the night. When the archbishop of Canterbury died, the king wanted the pope to give Thomas this position. It would just mean that Thomas would have to be ordained a priest. But Thomas told him plainly that he did not want to be the archbishop of Canterbury. He realized that being in that position would put him in direct conflict with Henry II. Thomas knew that he would have to defend the Church and that would mean trouble. "Your affection for me would turn into hatred," he warned Henry. The king paid no attention and Thomas was made a priest and a bishop in 1162. At first, things went along as well as ever. All too soon, however, the king began to demand money which Thomas felt he could not rightly take from the Church. The king grew more and more angry with his former friend. Finally, he began to treat Thomas harshly. For a while, Thomas was tempted to give in a bit. Then he began to realize just how much Henry hoped to control the Church. Thomas was very sorry that he had even thought of giving in to the king. He did penance for his weakness, and ever after held firm.

One day, the king was very angry. "Will no one rid me of this archbishop?" Some of his knights took him seriously. They went off to murder the archbishop. They attacked him in his own cathedral. He died, saying, "For the name of Jesus and in defense of the Church, I am willing to die." It was December 29, 1170. The entire Christian world was horrified at such a crime. Pope Alexander III held the king personally responsible for the murder. Miracles began to happen at Thomas' tomb. He was proclaimed a saint by the same pope in 1173.

Thomas Becket grew spiritually as he went through life. He teaches us that we can grow spiritually, too, if we pray and live a sacrificing life. We can ask him to help us.

DECEMBER 30

ST. ANYSIA

Anysia lived in Thessalonica toward the end of the second century. Thessalonica was an ancient city to which St. Paul himself had first brought the faith of Jesus. Anysia was a Christian and after her parents' death, she used her good fortune to help the poor.

In her day, there was a cruel persecution of Christians in Thessalonica. The governor was especially determined to stop all Christians from meeting together for Mass. But Anysia started out one day to try to go to a Christian meeting. As she passed a certain gate, called Cassandra, a guard took notice of her. Stepping out in front of her, he demanded to know where she was going. Frightened, Anysia stepped backwards, tracing a cross on her forehead. At that, the soldier grabbed her and shook her roughly. "Who are you" he shouted. "And where are you going?" Anysia took a deep breath and replied, "I am a servant of Jesus Christ," she said. "I am going to the Lord's assembly."

"Oh yes?" sneered the guard. "I will stop that. I will take you to sacrifice to the gods. Today we worship the sun." At the same time, he snatched off her veil. Anysia put up a good struggle, and the pagan grew more and more furious. Finally, in a rage, he drew his sword and ran it through her. The saint fell dead at his feet. When the persecution ended, the Christians of Thessalonica built a church over the spot where St. Anysia had given her life for Christ. Anysia died around 304.

We may have noticed how many martyrs this book contains. There isn't an easy way to get to heaven. We see that following Jesus has to cost us something. Not everything in life will be be easy. We can ask St. Anysia to give us her courage and love for Jesus.

ST. SYLVESTER I

This pope dates back to early Christian times, to the reign of Constantine, in fact. Sylvester I became pope in 314 and he reigned until his death in 335—twenty-one years.

The story is told that Constantine had at first persecuted Pope Sylvester. The emperor contracted leprosy and was going to have a pagan ritual of some kind performed. He was desperate for a cure. It seems that Constantine had a dream in which St. Peter and St. Paul spoke to him. They told the emperor to go to Pope Sylvester for a cure. Constantine asked the pope to be baptized and he was, in the basilica of St. John Lateran. It was during the reception of Baptism that Constantine was completely cured. From then on, Constantine not only permitted the Christian religion to exist, but encouraged it.

Devotion to Pope Sylvester I was well-known during the early Church. He is the first pope not a martyr to be proclaimed a saint. In the basilica of St. John Lateran in Rome, an impressive mosaic decorates one wall. It shows Jesus giving keys of spiritual power to Pope St. Sylvester I.

On this last day of the year, we can ask Pope St. Sylvester I to take care of us, the Christians of today, the way he did when he lived on earth.

INDEX

*Alphabetial Listing by
First Nameof the Saints In Volumes I and II*

A

St. Achilleus - May 12 (volume 1)

St. Adelaide - December 16

St. Agatha - February 5 (volume 1)
patroness of the Island of Malta and of nurses

St. Agnes - January 21 (volume 1)
*patroness of chastity, of the Children of Mary and the
Girl Scouts*

St. Agnes of Montepulciano - April 20 (volume 1)

St. Aiden - August 31

St. Albert the Great - November 15
patron of medical technicians and scientists

All Saints' Day - November 1

All Souls' Day - November 2

St. Aloysius Gonsaga - June 21 (volume 1)
patron of youth

St. Alphonsus Liguori - August 1
patron of confessors

St. Alphonsus Rodriguez - October 30

St. Ambrose - December 7
patron of candle-makers, candle-sellers and of learning

Bl. Andre Bessette - January 6 (volume 1)

St. Andrew - November 30
*patron of Scotland and Russia, of single women,
of fishermen*

341

St. Andrew Dung-Lac and Companions -November 24

St. Andrew Fournet - May 13 (volume 1)

St. Andrew Kim Taegon and St. Paul Chong Hasang - September 20

St. Angela Merici - January 27 (volume 1)

St. Anne and St. Joachim - July 26
St. Anne: patroness of Canada, of mothers, grand-mothers, homemakers, and of cabinet-makers

Bl. Anne of St. Bartholomew - June 7 (volume 1)

Annunciation of the Lord - March 25 (volume 1)

St. Anselm - April 21 (volume 1)

St. Anthony Claret - October 24

St. Anthony Mary Zaccaria - July 5

Bl. Anthony Neyrot - April 10 (volume 1)

St. Anthony of Egypt - January 17 (volume 1)
patron of grave diggers, butchers, basket and brush makers

St. Anthony of Padua - June 13 (volume 1)
patron of finding lost articles, of the poor, of childless married women, of cemetery workers

St. Antoninus - May 10 (volume 1)

St. Anysia - December 30

St. Apollonia and the Martyrs of Alexandria - February 9 (volume 1)
patroness of dentists and prayed to for tooth aches

Assumption of the Blessed Virgin Mary - August 15

St. Athanasius - May 2 (volume 1)

St. Augustine - August 28
patron of theologians, printers and brewers

St. Augustine of Canterbury - May 27 (volume 1)
patron of England

B

St. Barachisius and St. Jonas - March 29 (volume 1)

St. Barbatus - February 19 (volume 1)

St. Barnabas - June 11 (volume 1)
patron of Antioch

St. Bartholomew - August 24
patron of plasterers

St. Basil and St. Gregory Nazianzen - January 2
(volume 1)
St. Basil: patron of hospital administrators

St. Basilissa and St. Julian - January 9 (volume 1)

St. Bathildis - January 30 (volume 1)

Venerable Bede - May 25 (volume 1)

Beheading of St. John the Baptist - August 29

St. Benedict - July 11
*co-patron of Europe with St. Cyril and St. Methodius,
patron of monks and protector against poisoning*

St. Benedict Joseph Labre - April 16 (volume 1)
patron of homeless people

St. Berard and Companions - January 16 (volume 1)

St. Bernadette - February 18 (volume 1)
*patroness of victims of asthma and children
of alcoholic parents*

St. Bernard - August 20
patron of candle makers

St. Bernardine of Siena - May 20 (volume 1)
*patron of advertisers, media personnel; people in public
relations and prayed to by or for people addicted to
gambling*

St. Bertilla - November 5

Bl. Bertrand - September 6

St. Bibiana - December 2

Birth of the Blessed Virgin Mary - September 8

Birth of John the Baptist - June 24 (volume 1)

St. Blase - February 3 (volume 1)
patron and protector against throat ailments

St. Botvid - July 28

St. Bonaventure - July 15

St. Boniface - June 5 (volume 1)
patron of Germany

St. Boris and St. Gleb - July 24

St. Bridget of Sweden - July 23
patroness of Sweden

St. Brigid of Ireland - February 1 (volume 1)
*patroness of Ireland, of newborn babies and of
dairy workers*

St. Bruno - October 6
patron of priests who expel demons (exorcists)

C

St. Caesarius of Nazianzen - February 25 (volume 1)

St. Caius and St. Soter - April 22 (volume 1)

St. Cajetan - August 7

St. Callistus I - October 14

St. Canute - January 19 (volume 1)

St. Casimir - March 4 (volume 1)
patron of Poland

St. Catherine Laboure - November 28

St. Catherine of Ricci - February 13 (volume 1)

St. Catherine of Siena - April 29 (volume 1)
patroness of Italy, of nurses and of fire prevention

St. Catherine of Alexandria - November 25
*patroness of philosophers, jurists, teachers,
students, and wheel-makers*

Bl. Catherine of St. Augustine - May 8 (volume 1)

St. Cecilia - November 22
*patroness of musicians, of poets, singers and
organ-builders*

St. Celestine V - May 19 (volume 1)
patron of bookbinders

St. Chaeremon and St. Ischyrion - December 22

Chair of St. Peter - February 22 (volume 1)

St. Charbel - December 24

St. Charles Borromeo - November 4
patron of catechists

St. Charles Lwanga and Companions-June 3 (volume 1)
St. Charles Lwanga: patron of black African children

Bl. Charles the Good - March 2 (volume 1)

Christmas, the Birthday of Jesus - December 25

Bl. Christina - January 18 (volume 1)

St. Clare - August 11
patroness of television

St. Colette - March 6 (volume 1)

St. Columban - November 23
patron of Ireland and Irish monks

Bl. Contardo Ferrini - October 27
patron of universities

Conversion of St. Paul - January 25 (volume 1)

St. Cornelius and St. Cyprian - September 16

St. Cosmas and St. Damian - September 26
patrons of surgeons, barbers, doctors and pharmacists

St. Cuthbert - March 20 (volume 1)
patron of sailors

St. Cyril and St. Methodius - February 14 (volume 1)
co-patrons of Europe along with St. Benedict

St. Cyril of Alexandria - June 27 (volume 1)

St. Cyril of Jerusalem - March 18 (volume 1)

D

St. Damasus I - December 11

Bl. Damien of Molokai - April 15 (volume 1)

St. David I of Scotland - May 24 (volume 1)

St. Denis and Companions - October 9

St. Deogratias - March 22 (volume 1)

Bl. Didacus - March 24 (volume 1)

St. Dominic - August 8
patron of astronomers

St. Dominic of Silos - December 20

St. Dominic Savio - March 9 (volume 1)
patron of choir boys

E

St. Eanswida - September 12

St. Edmund - November 20

St. Edmund Campion - December 1

St. Edward - October 13

Eleven Martyrs of Almeria, Spain - October 10

St. Elizabeth Ann Seton - January 4 (volume 1)

St. Elizabeth Bichier - August 26

St. Elizabeth of Hungary - November 17
patroness of third order members, of bakers, of soup kitchens and shelters

St. Elizabeth of Portugal - July 4

St. Emily de Vialar - June 17 (volume 1)

St. Ephrem - June 9 (volume 1)

St. Eucherius - February 20 (volume 1)

Bl. Eugene de Mazenod - May 21 (volume 1)

Bl. Eugene III - July 8

St. Eulogius of Spain - March 11 (volume 1)

St. Euphrasia - March 13 (volume 1)

St. Eusebius - August 2

St. Evaristus - October 26

F

St. Fabian and St. Sebastian - January 20 (volume 1)

St. Faustina and St. Jovita - February 15 (volume 1)
patrons of the city of Brescia

St. Felicity and St. Perpetua - March 7 (volume 1)
St. Felicity: patroness of motherhood

St. Felicity and her Seven Sons - July 10

St. Felix and St. Cyprian - October 12

St. Felix II - March 1 (volume 1)

St. Fidelis of Sigmaringen - April 24 (volume 1)

St. Fina (Seraphina) - March 12 (volume 1)

First Martyrs of the Church of Rome - June 30
(volume 1)

St. Flannan - December 18

St. Flora of Beaulieu - October 5

St. Foillan - October 31

St. Frances of Rome - March 9 (volume 1)
patroness of motorists along with St. Christopher

Bl. Francis Anthony of Lucera - November 29

St. Francis Caracciolo - June 4 (volume 1)

St. Francis de Sales - January 24 (volume 1)
patron of authors, journalists and deaf people

St. Frances Xavier Cabrini - November 13
*patroness of immigrants, emigrants and hospital
administrators*

St. Francis of Assisi - October 4
*patron of Italy, of Catholic Action, of merchants,
ecologists and animals*

St. Francis of Paola - April 2 (volume 1)
patron of seamen

St. Francis Xavier - December 3
*patron of missionaries, of the Apostleship of Prayer, of
Borneo, Australia, New Zealand and China*

Bl. Francois de Montmorency Laval - May 6 (volume 1)

Bl. Frederic Janssoone - August 5

St. Frederick - July 18

G

St. Gabriel, St. Michael and St. Raphael - September 29
*St. Gabriel: patron of radio, television, telephone workers
and mail carriers*

St. Gabriel of Our Lady of Sorrows - February 27
(volume 1)
patron of seminarians and youth

St. Genevieve - January 3 (volume 1)
patroness of Paris

St. George - April 23.(volume 1)
*patron of England, of soldiers, of farmers and
of Boy Scouts*

St. Gerard of Brogne - October 3

St. Germaine of Pibrac - June 15 (volume 1)
patroness of sheep herders

St. Gertrude - November 16
patroness of the West Indies

St. Gildas - January 29 (volume 1)

St. Giles - September 1
*patron of crippled people, homeless people and
blacksmiths*

Bl. Giles Mary - February 7 (volume 1)

St. Godfrey - November 8

Bl. Gregory Barbarigo - June 18 (volume 1)

St. Gregory Nazianzen and St. Basil the Great -
January 2 (volume 1)

St. Gregory the Great - September 3
patron of England and of teachers

St. Gregory VII - May 25 (volume 1)

Guardian Angels - October 2

H

Bl. Henry of Treviso - June 10 (volume 1)

St. Henry II - July 13
patron of Benedictine Oblates

St. Hilarion - October 21

St. Hilary of Poitiers - January 13 (volume 1)
patron and protector against snake bites

St. Hippolytus and St. Pontian - August 13

The Holy Innocents - December 28

St. Hugh of Grenoble - April 1 (volume 1)

I

St. Ignatius of Antioch - October 17

St. Ignatius of Laconi - May 11 (volume 1)

St. Ignatius of Loyola - July 31
patron of retreats and of soldiers

Immaculate Conception of Mary - December 8

St. Irenaeus - June 28 (volume 1)

St. Isaac Jogues, St. John deBrebeuf and Companions -
October 19

St. Isidore of Seville - April 4 (volume 1)

St. Isidore the Farmer - May 15 (volume 1)
patron of farmers

J

St. James the apostle - July 25
patron of pharmacists, pilgrims, victims of arthritis,
manual laborers, hat makers and patron of Spain
and Chile

St. James and St. Philip apostles - May 3 (volume 1)

Bl. James Duckett - April 19 (volume 1)

St. James Intercisus - November 27

St. Jane Frances de Chantal - August 18 in U.S.A.
patroness of hunters

St. Jane Valois - February 4 (volume 1)

St. Januarius - September 19
patron of blood banks

St. Jerome - September 30
patron of librarians

St. Jerome Emiliani - February 8 (volume 1)
patron of orphans and homeless children

St. Joachim and St. Anne - July 26
St. Joachim: patron of grandfathers

Bl. Joan Delanoe - August 17

St. Joan of Arc - May 30 (volume 1)
patron of France, of virgins, service women and soldiers

Bl. Joan of Toulouse - March 31 (volume 1)

St. John Baptist de la Salle - April 7 (volume 1)
patron of teachers

St. John Baptist Rossi - May 23 (volume 1)

St. John Berchmans - November 26
patron of students and altar boys

St. John Bosco - January 31 (volume 1)
patron of editors and of laborers

St. John Capistrano - October 23
patron of jurists and military chaplains

St. John Chrysostom - September 13
patron of preachers

St. John Climacus - March 30 (volume 1)

St. John Damascene - December 4

St. John de Brebeuf, St. Isaac Jogues and
Companions - October 19

Bl. John Duckett and Bl. Ralph Corby - September 7

St. John DuLac and the September Martyrs -September 2

St. John Eudes - August 19

St. John Fisher and St. Thomas More - June 22(volume 1)

St. John Francis Regis - June 16 (volume 1)
patron of medical social workers

St. John I - May 18 (volume 1)

St. John Gaulbert - July 12
patron of forest workers

St. John Kanty - December 23

St. John Joseph of the Cross - March 5 (volume 1)

• St. John Leonardi - October 9

St. John Neumann - January 5 (volume 1)

St. John of Egypt - March 27 (volume 1)

St. John of God - March 8 (volume 1)
*patron of hospitals, of the sick, of heart patients,
of nurses and of book sellers*

Bl. John of Rieti - August 9

St. John of Sahagun - June 12 (volume 1)

St. John of the Cross - December 14

St. John Roberts - December 10

St. John the Almsgiver - January 23 (volume 1)

St. John the Apostle - December 27
patron of Asia Minor

St. John Vianney - August 4
patron of parish priests

St. Jonas and St. Barachisius - March 29 (volume 1)

St. Josaphat - November 12

St. Joseph - March 19 (volume 1)
*patron of the Universal Church, of the dying, of
families, of carpenters, of providing for spiritual and
physical needs*

St. Joseph the Worker - May 1 (volume 1)
patron of workers

St. Joseph Barsabbas - July 20

St. Joseph Cafasso - June 23 (volume 1)
patron of prisoners

St. Joseph Calasanz - August 25
patron of Christian schools

St. Joseph Cupertino - September 18
patron of aviators

St. Joseph Moscati - April 12 (volume 1)

St. Jovita and St. Faustinus - February 15 (volume 1)
patrons of the city of Brescia

Bl. Juan Diego - December 9

St. Jude and St. Simon - October 28
*St. Jude: patron of impossible, desperate cases
and of hospitals*

St. Judith of Prussia - May 5 (volume 1)

St. Julian and St. Basilissa - January 9 (volume 1)

St. Julie Billiart - April 8 (volume 1)

Bl. Junipero Serra - July 1

St. Justin - June 1 (volume 1)
patron of philosophers

K

Bl. Kateri Tekakwitha - July 14
patroness of Native Americans

Bl. Katharine Drexel - March 3 (volume 1)

St. Kenneth - October 11

L

Bl. Lawrence Humphrey, Bl. Roger Dickenson,
Bl. Ralph Milner - July 7

St. Lawrence - August 10
patron of cooks and the poor

St. Lawrence Brindisi - July 21

St. Lawrence Justinian - September 5

St. Lawrence O'Toole - November 14

St. Lawrence Ruiz and Companions - September 28

St. Leo IV - July 17

St. Leo the Great - November 10

Bl. Lidwina - April 14 (volume 1)
patroness of skaters

St. Louis of France - August 25
patron of third order members and of barbers

Bl. Louis of Thuringia - September 11

St. Lucius, St. Montanus and Companions - February 24 (volume 1)

St. Lucy - December 13
patroness of people with eye diseases

St. Ludger - March 26 (volume 1)

St. Luke - October 18
patron of medical doctors, painters, glass-workers and brewers

St. Lupicinus and St. Romanus - February 28 (volume 1)

M

St. Macrina - January 14 (volume 1)

St. Marcellinus and St. Peter - June 2 (volume 1)

Bl. Margaret Pole - May 28 (volume 1)

St. Margaret Mary - October 16
apostle of the Sacred Heart

St. Margaret of Scotland - November 16
patroness of learning

St. Marguerite Bourgeoys - January 12 (volume 1)
Bl. Marguerite D'Youville - December 23
St. Maria Goretti - July 6
patroness of virgins, of chastity and of the Children of Mary

Bl. Marie-Leonie Paradis - May 4 (volume 1)
Bl. Marie Rose Durocher - October 6
St. Mark the Evangelist - April 25 (volume 1)
patron of notaries

St. Martha - July 29
patroness of cooks, domestic servants, hospital dietitians and inn keepers

St. Martin de Porres - November 3
  patron of Black Americans and hair dressers

St. Martin I - April 13 (volume 1)

St. Martin of Tours - November 11
  patron of the homeless and of soldiers

Martyrs of Orange - July 9

St. Mary Magdalene - July 22

St. Mary Magdalen de Pazzi - May 25 (volume 1)

Bl. Mary of the Incarnation - April 18 (volume 1)
Mary, Mother of God - January 1 (volume 1)
Mary, our Queen - August 22
St. Matthew - September 21
  patron of bankers, tax collectors and accountants
St. Matilda - March 14 (volume 1)

St. Matthias - May 14 (volume 1)

St. Maximilian Kolbe - August 14

St. Maximinius - May 29 (volume 1)

St. Meletius - February 12 (volume 1)

St. Methodius and St. Cyril - February 14 (volume 1)

St. Methodius I- June 14 (volume 1)

St. Michael, St. Gabriel, St. Raphael - September 29
  *St. Michael: patron of France, of radiologists, of persons
  in battle, of paratroopers, of grocers, of mariners and
  helper in temptation*

Bl. Michelina - June 20 (volume 1)

Bl. Miguel Augustin Pro - November 23

St. Monica - August 27
  patroness of mothers and converts

St. Montanus, St. Lucius and Companions-
February 24 (volume 1)

N

St. Narcissus - October 29

St. Nereus and Achilleus - May 12 (volume 1)

St. Nersus - November 19

St. Nicholas - December 6
patron of children, of sailors, of bakers, of
merchants, of prisoners, of Greece and co-patron with
St. Andrew of Russia

Bl. Nicholas Albergati - May 9 (volume 1)

St. Nicholas Tolentino - September 10
patron of mariners

St. Nino - December 15

St. Norbert - June 6 (volume 1)

Bl. Notker - April 6 (volume 1)

O

St. Olympias - December 17

St. Onesimus - February 16 (volume 1)

St. Otto - July 2

Our Lady of Guadalupe - December 12
patroness of Mexico, Latin America and the
Philippines

Our Lady of Lourdes - February 11 (volume 1)

Our Lady of Mount Carmel - July 16

Our Lady of Sorrows - September 15

Our Lady of the Holy Rosary - October 7

P/Q

St. Pacificus - September 24

St. Pammachius - August 30

St. Pancras - May 12 (volume 1)

St. Pantaleon - July 27
patron of doctors

St. Paschal Baylon - May 17 (volume 1)
patron of Eucharistic congresses and
Eucharistic societies

St. Patrick - March 17 (volume 1)
patron of Ireland

St. Paul - January 25/June 29 (volume 1)
patron of Malta, of journalists and of hospital public relations

Conversion of - January 25

St. Paul and St. Peter - June 29

St. Paulinus of Nola - June 22 (volume 1)

St. Paul Miki and Companions - February 6 (volume 1)

St. Paul of the Cross - October 19

St. Paul the Hermit - January 15 (volume 1)
patron of weavers

St. Pelagius - June 26 (volume 1)

St. Perpetua and St. Felicity - March 7 (volume 1)

St. Peter and St. Marcellinus- June 2 (volume 1)

St. Peter and St. Paul - June 29 (volume 1)
St. Peter: patron of fishermen

St. Peter Canisius - December 21
patron of Germany

St. Peter Chanel - April 28 (volume 1)

St. Peter Claver - September 9
patron of Colombia and of Black Catholic missions

St. Peter Damian - February 21 (volume 1)

St. Peter Julian Eymard - August 3

St. Philip and St. James - May 3 (volume 1)

St. Philip Neri - May 26 (volume 1)
patron of Rome and of teenagers

St. Pius V - April 30 (volume 1)

St. Pius X - August 21

St. Polycarp - February 23 (volume 1)

St. Pontian and St. Hippolytus - August 13

St. Porcarius and Companions - August 12

St. Porphyry - February 26 (volume 1)

Presentation of Mary - November 21

Presentation of the Lord - February 2 (volume 1)

R

St. Radbertus - April 26 (volume 1)

Bl. Ralph Corby and Bl. John Duckett - September 7

St. Raphael, St. Michael and St. Gabriel - September 29
*St. Raphael: patron of blind people, of doctors, nurses,
lovers, travelers and of happy endings*

St. Raymond of Penyafort - January 7 (volume 1)
*patron of Church lawyers and of librarians of
medical records*

Bl. Richard Gwyn - October 25

St. Richard of Chichester - April 3 (volume 1)

St. Rita of Cascia - May 22 (volume 1)
patroness of impossible cases

St. Robert Bellarmine - September 17
patron of catechists

Bl. Roger Dickenson, Bl. Ralph Milner, Bl. Lawrence
Humphrey - July 7

St. Romanus and Lupicinus - February 28 (volume 1)

St. Romuald - June 19 (volume 1)

St. Rose of Lima - August 23
*patroness of the Americas, the Philippines and
the West Indies*

St. Rose of Viterbo - September 4

St. Rose Philippine Duchesne - November 18

Bl. Rose Venerini - May 7 (volume 1)

S

St. Sabas - December 5

St. Scholastica - February 10 (volume 1)
patroness and protector against convulsions in children

St. Sebastian - January 20 (volume 1)
patron of athletes and archers

St. Serapion - March 21 (volume 1)

St. Sergius - September 25

Seven Holy Founders of the Servite Order - February 17 (volume 1)

St. Simeon - October 8

St. Simon and St. Jude - October 28

St. Simplicius - March 10 (volume 1)

St. Sixtus II and Companions - August 7

St. Soter and St. Caius - April 22 (volume 1)

St. Stanislaus - April 11 (volume 1)
patron of Poland and of receiving the Anointing of the Sick

St. Stephen - December 26
patron of stonemasons and bricklayers

St. Stephen Harding - April 17 (volume 1)

St. Stephen of Hungary - August 16
patron of Hungary

St. Sylvester I - December 31

T

St. Teresa of Avila - October 15
protector against headaches

St. Thecla - September 23

St. Theodore Tiro - November 9

St. Theodosius - January 11 (volume 1)

St. Theophane Venard - November 6

St. Theresa of the Child Jesus - October 1
patroness of missionaries, of tuberculosis patients, of aviators and of florists

St. Thomas, apostle - July 3
patron of the East Indies and of architects

St. Thomas Aquinas - January 28 (volume 1)
  universal patron of universities, colleges and schools

St. Thomas Becket - January 29 (volume 1)

St. Thomas More and St. John Fisher - June 22(volume 1)
  St. Thomas More: patron of lawyers

St. Thomas of Villanova - September 22

St. Thorfinn - January 8 (volume 1)

St. Timothy and St. Titus - January 26 (volume 1)
  *St. Timothy: patron and protector against
  stomach disorders*

Bl. Timothy Giaccardo - October 22
  patron of media evangelizers

St. Titus and St. Timothy - January 26 (volume 1)
  St. Titus: patron of Crete

Bl. Torello - March 16 (volume 1)

The Transfiguration - August 6

Triumph of the Holy Cross - September 14

St. Turibius of Mongrovejo - March 23 (volume 1)

St. Tutilo - March 28 (volume 1)

U

St. Ubald - May 16 (volume 1)

Bl. Urban V - December 19

V

St. Vincent de Paul - September 27
  patron of charitable institutions

St. Vincent Ferrer - April 5 (volume 1)
patron of builders

St. Vincent of Saragossa - January 22 (volume 1)
  patron of wine growers

Visitation of Mary - May 31 (volume 1)

W

St. Waldetrudis - April 9 (volume 1)
St. William - January 10 (volume 1)
St. William of Monte Vergine - June 25 (volume 1)
St. William of York - June 28 (volume 1)
St. Willibrord - November 7
  patron of Holland and of epileptics

X/Y/Z

St. Zachary - March 15 (volume 1)
St. Zita - April 27 (volume 1)
  patroness of housekeepers and maids

auline BOOKS & MEDIA

CALIFORNIA
3908 Sepulveda Blvd., Culver City, CA 90230; 310-397-8676
5945 Balboa Ave., San Diego, CA 92111; 619-565-9181
46 Geary Street, San Francisco, CA 94108; 415-781-5180

FLORIDA
145 S.W. 107th Ave., Miami, FL 33174; 305-559-6715

HAWAII
1143 Bishop Street, Honolulu, HI 96813; 808-521-2731

ILLINOIS
172 North Michigan Ave., Chicago, IL 60601; 312-346-4228

LOUISIANA
4403 Veterans Memorial Blvd., Metairie, LA 70006; 504-887-7631

MASSACHUSETTS
50 St. Paul's Ave., Jamaica Plain, Boston, MA 02130; 617-522-8911
Rte. 1, 885 Providence Hwy., Dedham, MA 02026; 617-326-5385

MISSOURI
9804 Watson Rd., St. Louis, MO 63126; 314-965-3512

NEW JERSEY
561 U.S. Route 1, Wick Plaza, Edison, NJ 08817; 908-572-1200

NEW YORK
150 East 52nd Street, New York, NY 10022; 212-754-1110
78 Fort Place, Staten Island, NY 10301; 718-447-5071

OHIO
2105 Ontario Street, Cleveland, OH 44115; 216-621-9427

PENNSYLVANIA
9171-A Roosevelt Blvd., Philadelphia, PA
19114; 215-676-9494

SOUTH CAROLINA
243 King Street, Charleston, SC 29401; 803-577-0175

TENNESSEE
4811 Poplar Ave., Memphis, TN 38117; 901-761-2987

TEXAS
114 Main Plaza, San Antonio, TX 78205; 210-224-8101

VIRGINIA
1025 King Street, Alexandria, VA 22314; 703-549-3806

CANADA
3022 Dufferin Street, Toronto, Ontario, Canada M6B 3T5; 416-781-9131
1155 Yonge Street, Toronto, Ontario, Canada M4T 1W2; 416-934-3440